sell sell sell

Barry Bearden

THE
ARCHANGELS'
SHARE

The Story of the World's Oldest
Business Angels Syndicate

by
Kenny Kemp, Graham Lironi
& Peter Shakeshaft

With a foreword by
Sir Brian Souter

Saraband

Published by Saraband
Digital World Centre
1 Lowry Plaza
The Quays
Salford
M50 3UB

www.saraband.net

The opinions expressed in this book reflect the views of
Mike Rutterford and Barry Sealey as voiced to the authors
during interviews in the preparation of this book.

ISBN: 9781910192894
ebook: 9781910192900

Printed and bound in Great Britain by Clays Ltd, St Ives plc.

MIX
Paper from
responsible sources
FSC® C018072

FOREWORD

I can hardly believe it is 25 years ago since Barry Sealey explained to me his intention to support Scottish businesses that were often no more than a glimmer in the eye. He had joined the board of Stagecoach as a non-executive director with a wealth of experience and common sense about business. My sister Ann Gloag and I welcomed his insight, his sense of humour and his company. He had already asked me to support a couple of companies, which we did, but when he told Ann and I that he and Mike Rutterford were planning to do something more for young companies in Scotland, I said we would be happy to help.

Barry and Mike never waste an opportunity. It wasn't long after this that we were invited to put money into a laser eye-testing machine, which was then a brilliant new concept from Douglas Anderson. We knew it would be high risk – and that all the money might be lost. Nevertheless, we helped with funding for the first prototype. We knew that if Barry, Mike and Sir Gerald Elliot were prepared to back it, then we would put some money in too. Eventually, after many rounds of investment, Optos turned out to be a winner for Archangels, and for Scotland. Since then, we have watched with great admiration as Archangels, a unique syndicate now revered around the world, has grown and developed. Today, its chairman is Eric Young and it has a professional executive team examining the investment portfolio and trying to identify winners. There are around 70 investors in the outer circle who are making a real difference with their support.

Scotland desperately needs organisations like Archangels to support enterprise, initiative and hard work. And it needs people who are prepared to take a calculated risk to build new companies in Scotland and make a bit of money in return. One thing I have learned in my business life: there is no guarantee for success. No one has a right to make it big. It requires application, tough choices and a sprinkling of luck. Our greatest challenge is 'fear of failure', an attitude that is holding us back as a nation. Archangels are brave individuals who overcome this fear and create opportunity. My sincerest congratulations to Archangels on its first 25 years. I'm sure some of the tales in this book will be enjoyed – and lessons learned. And here's to another 25 years and more: advising, supporting and growing winning businesses in Scotland.

Sir Brian Souter,
Chairman of Stagecoach Group Plc

Contents

PROLOGUE

"The United Kingdom has been the most active angel market in Europe with Scotland being particularly active."

'Financing High Growth Firms: The Role of Angel Investors',
OECD, Paris 2011

In recent years it has become clear that Scotland leads the way in angel investment, not only in Europe but throughout the world. So why is this? There are clearly a number of contributing factors, but this book explores probably the most important of all: the founding in 1992 of Archangels by two men who have shown extraordinary energy, passion and skill in building what is now the oldest and one of the biggest business angel syndicates in the world. An amazing feat, particularly given that, at the start, they didn't even know they were angels and they certainly had no vision or ambition to create such an organisation.

This book uncovers the unique and lasting business relationship between Barry Sealey and Mike Rutterford and follows their journey to the present day. It tells of successes and failures along the way; explores the learning curve both of early-stage investment and the formation of a successful business angel syndicate; introduces the other key characters and organisations involved in the journey and helps to explain why Scotland has emerged as a global leader in angel investing.

Archangels has led investment of more than £220 million into some 80 early-stage companies in Scotland of which just over £100 million has come from the pockets of Barry, Mike and the other syndicate members. But Archangels is not only about money. The other key ingredient of the investment process is the huge level of help, advice and connections that the syndicate can bring to its young companies. This is the real strength of angel investing and this book relates the tales of success and failure from all viewpoints.

There are of course other key players and organisations in Scotland who have played an important part in the encouragement of business angels. Sandy Finlayson, a lawyer with MBM Commercial, has played a crucial role. David Grahame, the chief executive of LINC Scotland, has been pivotal in creating the right environment. The creation of the Scottish Co-investment Fund in 2003 was a bold and wonderfully encouraging move. And there are many others. The part that they have all played and their interaction with Archangels will be explored and, gradually, it might become clear why Scotland is a world leader in this field.

This is the story of a group of Scotland-based individuals who have created a distinct international phenomenon: the angel investment syndicate. Independent academics and investment professionals recognise Archangels as the oldest syndicate of business angel investors in the world. But, at its heart, this story is about two extraordinary men who didn't know each other and who had both made enough money after very busy business lives to retire, relax and enjoy the fruits of their success. They chose to do otherwise, and Scotland is the richer for their decisions.

While today Archangels is a renowned investment syndicate with national stature and international recognition, it is largely unrecognisable from its foundation nearly 25 years ago, so the tale of how Barry Sealey and Mike Rutterford joined forces and brought to life a distinct activity, based as much on personal relationships and human intuition as it is on raw financial figures and future sales projections, is worth recounting in some detail.

Together Barry and Mike were the unwitting progenitors of the 'Scottish Model', hands-in-their-pocket investors who have proven how business angels operate most successfully as a syndicate of like-minded individuals.

1

THE BIRTH OF ARCHANGELS

"It is astounding that however culturally, educationally and socially different they are as individuals, they have this ability to trust each other, which is unfathomable to many people."

Juliette Chapman,
Gatekeeper of Archangels, 1994–1999

Economically, 1992 was a very difficult year in the UK. There were real fears that the country was heading for another Great Depression with GDP at -0.7%, interest rates at 9% and unemployment over 7% with nearly three million people out of work. The pound was being battered by the strong dollar and on 16 September 1992, known as Black Wednesday, currency speculators forced Britain to suspend its membership of the exchange rate mechanism (ERM) despite extreme government action that day to raise interest rates to 15% in an effort to avoid the inevitable.

It was also a hard time for dealmakers on both Wall Street and in the City of London. Recession had made the big takeover bids, and the massive fees that went with them, extremely rare.

"It was grim at the time in Edinburgh," recalled Mike Rutterford. "In 1992, you could stand at one end of Queen Street and you could hardly see the facade of the buildings for the 'For Sale' signs, and even in George Street it was very depressing. You could buy Georgian properties in Melville Street for tuppence ha'penny, but the problem was you couldn't find tenants, and the cost of money was prohibitive."

It was against this background, in June of that year, that Barry Sealey and Mike Rutterford met for the first time and sketched out an informal agreement to work together. This agreement would lead to the development of Archangels, though neither man had the slightest inkling of what lay ahead.

Born in Bristol in 1936, to parents who encouraged an interest in practical learning, Barry Sealey attended Dursley Grammar School before gaining a place at St John's, Cambridge, to read natural sciences and engineering, winning the Hocking class prize for physics in his third year. Barry's interests were more inclined towards industry than further academia and in 1958, as a result of a successful interview with the chairman, Harold Salvesen, he joined the whaling and transport company Christian Salvesen as a management trainee.

Salvesen management trainees were expected to spend time understanding the business from the bottom up, which for Barry meant spending time at sea on the fishing boats as well as in the administrative offices of the fleet. This appealed to Barry's practical manner and reinforced his natural interest in the science and engineering aspects that underpin many businesses.

After marrying Helen in 1960, Barry continued to work his way up the Salvesen organisation in its Edinburgh head office.

This was a period of enormous change for Salvesen, as it moved into fish-freezing factory ships and land-based cold storage facilities and away from its original business of whaling. Seeing increasing potential in cold storage, in 1964 Salvesen bought a Swedish-owned cold store in Grimsby that operated alongside its own, installing Barry as manager of the combined operation.

In January 1968, Barry attended the Harvard Business School, supported by Christian Salvesen, subsequently returning to the Edinburgh headquarters and still focused on cold storage. During one of his many journeys from Edinburgh to Grimsby, Barry learned that Marks & Spencer was planning to go into frozen food and so arranged a meeting with the director of the food division, successfully selling them the Salvesen storage and distribution capability that was to support the M&S focus on quality. By 1973 Barry was on the main board and Salvesen was on its way to becoming a major player in the UK's frozen food industry.

Throughout the 1970s, Salvesen continued to diversify, building specialised ships for drilling and exploration and oil services. During this period Barry was at the front of many of the negotiations, using both his business and technical expertise to the full. In 1981 he became the group managing director and during the 1980s led a strategic move into the USA and oversaw the acquisition of Aggreko.

In 1990, after more than 30 years in the company, ten of which were as Managing Director, Barry retired from Salvesen, leaving behind an organisation fundamentally different from the one he had joined.

Retiring at the relatively youthful age of 54, having built up a comfortable capital sum and pension, Barry might have justifiably hung up his boots. But he is not that kind of man. He was quickly snapped up to sit on various boards and, on occasion, was minded to invest relatively modest sums of money into companies that, in his judgement, both deserved and needed it.

Born in Edinburgh in 1947, Mike Rutterford spent school holidays with his family on the Orkney island of Papa Westray, where he first developed his love of the sea. After a less than illustrious school career, he joined the Merchant Navy in 1964.

After five years with the Ben Line, working as third and then second mate on general cargo ships on the Far East trade routes, he decided to seek work ashore and, at around the time of his marriage to June, took a job in sales with the National Mutual Life Association of Australia at its Glasgow branch. Within two months he was the top salesman in Scotland and, by 1972, had been appointed manager of the Manchester office, the youngest of 16 managers across the UK.

In 1974 he moved back to Edinburgh and set up Rutterford Ltd, an insurance brokerage. The insurance brokerage dealt with both commercial and personal clients and, as part of the natural extension of the business, Mike increasingly began to operate as a broker for mortgage businesses.

This period was the start of the Edinburgh property boom and so, in 1977, he took the next natural step and set up an estate agency, Stuart Wyse Ogilvie (a name created to appeal to an aspirational market) with June Rutterford and Charles Brien as co-directors. Mike owned 87% of the company and was very much the driving force behind this new style of agency, continually reinvesting the profits into the business. The head office showroom was opened in George Street and looked very different from the usual property-selling environments of Edinburgh at a time when houses were traditionally sold through lawyers.

Previously in Edinburgh, 'For Sale' signs were not a common sight. The Rutterfords identified this as a real marketing opportunity, ensuring that the 'For Sale', 'Under Offer' and 'Sold' signboards of the company worked as their primary sales tools.

By 1985 company turnover had risen to £1.75 million and the firm had a network of 33 offices. In 1987 it was sold to GA in Scotland for £16 million, with Mike retained on a five-year contract and June on three years. Both were given seats on the board and Mike became one of the five UK directors who ran the sizeable UK-wide network of General Accident Property Services.

By 1991 he felt ready to leave the corporate life and left GA on amicable terms, keen to pursue his own business interests and spend more time with his family. He took a little time for reflection then began looking for opportunities that would allow him to invest some of his money and input his enormous talent for sales and management.

Mike and Barry came from very different backgrounds. Barry was the urbane epitome of very senior corporate life, an Englishman who had adopted Scotland (and been adopted by its people), comfortable in the company of his peers and widely respected. Mike was a swashbuckler and, in his own words, "a simple crofter from Leith" who had clawed his way to the top by building an estate agency at a time when the buying and selling of houses had been the principal preserve of the powerful legal fraternity in Scotland.

The common link for both men turned out to be a Scottish lawyer, Sandy Finlayson, who had worked with them both and finally introduced them to each other on 11 June 1992 at Mackenzies restaurant in Colinton. In addition to introducing Barry to Mike, Sandy's contribution to the support of early-stage companies in Scotland stretches much wider than just Archangels.

Sandy had studied law at Edinburgh University and became a partner in the legal firm of Fyfe Ireland, which later merged with the Glasgow firm Bird Semple. He was responsible for developing the fast-growing SME (small and medium-sized enterprises) market and began to champion early-stage companies. However, the merger of Bird Semple Fyfe Ireland was not a happy amalgamation and Sandy decided to leave in March 1993, joining Murray Beith Murray in October of that year.

But his abiding interest in young companies remained and, in 1993, he started up an informal advice network called The Business Forum where small companies could come and outline their challenges to an experienced audience who would then try and help with ideas and suggestions. It was enormously effective. Sandy was also becoming much more aware of the concept of business angels, which was emerging in the United States and he began to explore the possibilities of funding young companies through individual business angels. He also lobbied tirelessly for change to the financial regulations that made it an offence to pass round business plans, even between syndicate members. Sandy finally succeeded in this with the introduction of the Financial Services and Markets Act 2000, which introduced the concept of 'sophisticated investors' and 'high net worth individuals', which are now commonly used in all angel syndicates.

Within Murray Beith Murray, Sandy began to build a reputation for completing financing deals for young and emerging companies and brought in an associate, Stuart

Hendry, to help with the workload. Stuart was to become an expert practitioner on these deals and Peter Shakeshaft recalls completing some 100 deals with Stuart during his time as gatekeeper of Archangels.

In 2005, the young company and its angel legal work had grown to such an extent that Sandy, Stuart and one or two others took the brave step of buying out the commercial business of Murray Beith Murray to set up their own firm, MBM Commercial, to concentrate on that market.

Sandy has always been prominent in his support for innovation in Scotland and makes time to help and advise hopeful entrepreneurs. His reputation in the market extends far beyond Scotland's borders and he is undoubtedly one of the reasons for the success and global reputation of business angels in Scotland. His early experiences with Barry and Mike, and his subsequent close working relationship with Archangels, has been key to his ongoing involvement in the sector.

Sandy would continue to be a huge influence on the development of Archangels and the whole angel environment in Scotland, but not even he, as an astute lawyer, could foresee the importance of the introduction he had just made.

Barry took the initiative after that first meeting and invited Mike to meet with him at his modest office to explore whether there were any common interests in their respective ambitions. Here were two very different personalities, both strong and confident individuals, yet within a very short time they found a common purpose.

Within that first hour over a cup of coffee, they reached a general agreement. They wanted to help other Scottish companies get going and they set out, on a sheet of A4 paper, the guiding principles that would become the foundation of Scotland's first business angel syndicate, Archangels, although it would be some years before either of them realised what they had created that day.

There were four basic points on that sheet of paper:

1 – To put something back into Scotland by investing in young people and companies, particularly those in science and emerging technologies.
2 – To look for investments where they could add value by passing on their own business experience.
3 – To have fun.
4 – To make some money.

A quarter of a century later, these founding principles still apply within Archangels and remain the key foundations upon which Archangels operates.

"I remember that we agreed that we had both done well out of Scotland and we wanted to put something back," said Barry Sealey. "We agreed that one really good way of doing this would be to get involved with emerging technology companies. We agreed that we would put our own money in, but we also said we would put in our own time, effort and experience."

This last comment encapsulates the whole meaning of angel investing. Angel money is 'smart money'. The whole concept of angel investing is built around adding value to the company in which the angels have invested by bringing to bear the experience of the investors, introducing the company to the connections they need and effecting change when it is needed. Of course, this is beneficial to both the company and the angel investors, since 'added value' also means the opportunity of greater return for everybody involved.

So points one and two were relatively simple. Point three has often caused comment from serious investors, but, again, it is an essential part of the angel investing process. Both Barry and Mike had experienced a draining and exhausting corporate life that, although very successful, had ultimately led them to believe that life could be more exhilarating in the business environment and they really wanted to enjoy what they were doing. There would, of course, be many serious moments in the years ahead but there should and would be much time for great satisfaction in their successes and plenty of time for good-natured banter.

Point four seems obvious, but remarkably it was not, in the early stages, the driving force. Mike described making money from these investments as a good way of 'keeping the score' rather than a driving need to make money in its own right. But there is no doubt that this agreement between Barry and Mike was, when it came to deciding on any particular investment, nothing to do with philanthropy and all to do with the serious intent of making money, both for the investors and the founders. An early question from Barry to anybody who came with a business proposition was "How can we make a million pounds from this?" And woe betide anyone who couldn't answer that question.

And so, from that single short meeting, Archangels was born. A quarter of a century later, Archangels is renowned internationally.

2

THE EARLY DAYS

The term 'business angel' was not in common parlance in 1992, certainly not in Scotland. There were stirrings in the USA, and David Grahame in Scotland was beginning to devise a vehicle to encourage business angels, subsequently launched in 1993 as LINC Scotland. The concept of angels had been fairly well established in the theatre world, where groups of people would provide financing for a production and then hope to recoup that plus a modest profit from the subsequent box office receipts. Of course, if the production was a failure then box office receipts would be inadequate and the angels would lose out. A fitting simile for business angel investment!

What was certainly not established was the concept of angel syndicates, where a group of people would invest in the same company but act together under one code of conduct. John Waddell, a former chief executive of Archangels, saw some parallels with the opening for business of the Bank of Scotland in February 1696, established by the Scottish government to support Scottish business.

Research in the USA has suggested that the ideal geographical area for a successful angel investing community is around five million people. Scotland fits that concept neatly. John Waddell saw other characteristics that fitted the mould of angel investing: "I think what we were doing was catching a wave that has actually been going on in the New Town of Edinburgh, among merchants, financiers and lawyers, since it was built in the 1760s. There is an investing predisposition here in Scotland."

Mike and Barry had a number of tasks in front of them: they had to find suitable companies or ideas in which they could invest; they wanted to find a few like-minded people who might join them in those investments and they had to devise an investment agreement that would protect them, the founders and the company.

Since leaving Christian Salvesen, Barry had already made a few investments. He had invested in the Caledonian Brewing Company at the behest of Donald Macdonald and Sandy Orr and found he enjoyed his involvement. He followed this with small investments in Interface Graphics, a printing company; Addabox, a developer and producer of portable public address systems; motor vehicle seller George Thomson Brakeways; and steel tube manufacturer Wilson Byard. It was an eclectic bunch of companies made even more so by an investment in a small restaurant in Edinburgh's High Street called Les Partisans. Predictably, some of these companies eventually failed, although Caledonian Brewery remains a famous name to this day, having created one of Scotland's finest beers, Deuchars IPA.

Mike had also been thumbing his way through a few business plans but had found nothing that tickled his fancy. Once again it was Sandy Finlayson who began to introduce the real opportunities, which came to him through his growing interest in funding new companies and his increasing reputation as someone who could be approached with new ideas. Again, we have to bear in mind the gloomy economic climate in 1992 and the subsequent high cost of obtaining bank money to understand the need to find innovative ways to fund a business idea.

The first real breakthrough came in July 1992 when Sandy introduced Douglas Anderson, a creative industrial designer, to Barry. The result of that introduction would prove quite extraordinary in the story of Archangels, moving it from an initial investment by Barry, Mike and seven other individuals of £80,000 to a full stock market launch in February 2006 at an initial valuation of £165 million and its ultimate acquisition by Nikon in 2015 for £259 million. This is the story of Optos. The 14-year journey from initial investment to full flotation is simply remarkable and unlikely to be replicated anywhere in the world. It reflects huge leaps of faith by investors, dogged determination by its founder and simple hard work from all involved in the company.

Another individual who invested in the first round of Optos was Sir Gerald Elliot, who had been Barry's boss as chairman of Christian Salvesen and was knighted in 1986, the year after Christian Salvesen went public. A man with a razor-sharp intellect, he immediately understood what Barry and Mike were seeking to do. He became the third core member of Archangels and remained on the board until July 2003, investing both his money and his sage advice freely.

"For me, it was about supporting Scottish industry and industrial development," said Sir Gerald. "Of course, one of the advantages was the EIS tax relief. If you invested you could get remission of tax and this was also very interesting for us. We liked having this, but putting money back to help Scotland was the prime reason for me."

Another of those early investors in Optos was Robert Pattullo, who again had worked with Barry at Christian Salvesen and was later to join the executive team of Archangels as a key member of staff.

The next two most important investments were concluded on the same day in March 1993 and involved two companies in the emerging IT sector, Objective Software Technology (OST) and Solcom. Both sold out well, netting the investors significant profits and even allowing Mike to buy the yacht of his dreams from his share of the proceeds.

The story of OST represents a classic and highly successful angel investment. It is a first-class example of how angel investment should work, but rarely does!

In 1991 two young engineers, Eddie Anderson and Alan West, spun a business out of BT with the aim of developing a C++ software suite for use by computer programmers. Eddie and Alan were in their late 20s with little business experience, but were clearly very clever software engineers who had been working in BT research on emerging telecoms infrastructure.

Initially they approached Edinburgh & Lothian Enterprise and then Scottish Enterprise Lanarkshire, who were hugely supportive of the idea and indicated that they would be willing to invest £50,000 to get things started. However, in those days it was very difficult to access that kind of public money and the talks with Scottish Enterprise dragged on for many months, taking up a lot of management time with no guarantee of success at the end of the process.

Eventually, they were introduced to Barry and Mike through Sandy Finlayson and were invited to make a presentation – which was a disaster.

"In those days the processing power of computers was not a patch on today's computers. I lugged along a big PC unit with the keyboard while Alan carried the screen. We set it up for the demo that we had prepared and discovered I'd forgotten to take along the key that unlocked the keyboard!" recalled Eddie.

Not an auspicious start for a software company.

"Why don't you just tell us about your business?" asked Mike.

In the years to come, Barry and Mike never let Eddie and Alan forget their disastrous start. But the outcome of the presentation was promising and Barry and Mike agreed immediately to invest the £50,000 required, based on their assessment of Eddie and Alan and also the apparent encouragement from Scottish Enterprise that the products, if successfully developed, would be commercially viable.

That was the extent of the due diligence and meant, with Sandy's help on a relatively simple investment agreement, that the whole transaction was completed very quickly and cost-effectively. In March 1993, Barry, Mike, Sir Gerald and Brian Souter each put in £12,500, allowing the new company to develop its product to a commercial stage.

In fact, the timing was important as it allowed the product to be shown at the 1994 ObjectWorld trade show in Boston, where it won 'Best New Product' and attracted the attention of a number of the big global players in that sector. This was a crucial step and demonstrated the absolute importance of showcasing products on the world stage.

Mike took on the role of chairman to bring some much-needed business experience to the team and the company required two further tranches of investment: £30,000 in May 1995 and a final £52,000 in March 1996, making a total investment of £132,000 over the period. In January 1998, the company was sold to Wind River in the USA for £3.67 million, netting the investors a return of nearly 11 times their original investments and turning Eddie and Alan into millionaires.

"We were young and inexperienced guys. If we had known all the challenges I don't think we would have done it. It always takes longer than you think. You go into things with enthusiasm and you don't know what you don't know," reflected Eddie.

It was a genuine case of matching money, a good idea, committed management and business experience. Eddie and Alan continued working for Wind River for two years and then Eddie became a founding partner of Pentech Ventures LLP, a Scotland-based VC (venture capitalist) investing in technology companies in the UK and Ireland.

The first investment into Solcom Systems was made on the same day in March 1993 as the OST investment and, while it is a very different story, the eventual result was just as rewarding. It has to be said that good luck and good timing played an important part in the eventual outcome, but there was also typical perseverance and determination on the part of both the investors and the management team.

Solcom was a software and hardware developer that had, again like OST, sought funding from the local development agencies but was finding it hard to get a decision. The founding management team consisted of three clever guys, one of whom, Peter Wilson, would eventually become a serial investor in his own right. Sandy introduced the team to Barry and Mike, who decided they liked the look of both the product and the team and decided quickly to invest. Mike became chairman and the company began the task of commercialising its product, most significantly in the United States.

However, as with many development companies, things didn't run very smoothly. There was constant tension between the development team and the sales force, arising mainly from the desire of the sales force to meet the changing demands of their potential customers, while, at home, there was simply a desire to sell the product that had already been developed. Mike ran intensive strategy sessions with the team, which could be quite brutal but were aimed at getting everybody pointed in the same direction and concentrating on the commercial reality.

Some progress was being made when, out of the blue, Clydesdale Bank announced that it would be withdrawing its £400,000 facility and the investors were faced with a very tough decision. As chairman, it was effectively Mike's call as to whether to let the company go down or raise the necessary cash from the small investor base to keep going. Mike admits to some sleepless nights during that time, conscious that he was committing other people's cash as well as his own to an as-yet-unproven concept. It was a classic 50-50 decision, but eventually it was agreed to invest further and so the game began again.

But there was still a degree of dissent within the camp as to the best way forward, so Mike called in the services of Jim Mather, who had previously worked with IBM and had recently built up and sold the Computerland franchise in Scotland. Jim would subsequently become a Member of the Scottish Parliament and eventually Minister for Enterprise in the Scottish Nationalist Party government, but at that time he was the ideal guy to straighten out the team and he took on the task for a period of three months. In Mike's view, "The executives grew up. There was a board problem and Jim Mather, as a gentlemanly company doctor, was the mechanism to fix it. He did a bloody good job."

And so the company began to gain traction and caught the eye of ION Networks Inc., a USA-based software company quoted on the small-cap market but with aspirations to grow by acquisition, using its paper, and move onto the much more active NASDAQ market. It was a deal which took some nine months to complete and was in many ways not particularly attractive, but it was regarded by the investors and management as a get-out-of-jail-free card. Eventually, in November 1999, the deal was finalised, but not before the paper price was halved from its original worth of $4.56 per share to $2.28 per share. However, there was a collective sigh of relief that a solution had been found and a very small profit should be made.

Then came the dotcom boom and the NASDAQ market, to which ION had transferred on completion of the acquisition, simply took off. Within a few months the share price rose through the $10 mark and the investors, who had been embargoed from selling their shares for a period of time, obtained permission to begin selling. They sold some at $10, more at $14 and a further tranche at $20 but continued to sell as the shares reached a peak of $44. The market, of course, then went dramatically south as the dotcom bust hit hard and eventually ION shares fell to 16 cents.

Some of the investors and management team rode that particular tiger better than others, but Barry's records show that, for an investment of £75,895, he eventually realised £708,843, making a multiple of over nine times his investment. Mike got his yacht.

The completion of these first three investments also allowed the introduction of a simple standard investment agreement devised by Sandy, Barry and Mike. The initial investments in these companies were relatively modest and nobody wanted to see high, open-ended legal costs soaking up additional funds. The agreement that was crafted contained all the necessary protections for all of the parties and was sufficiently standard that it was 90% fit for purpose for all investments, leaving minimum room for negotiation or change.

"The fact that Mike and Barry were able to do these deals quickly and cheaply was critical to the success; the early deals gave it the traction," said Sandy.

The other feature of these deals was the remarkable lack of due diligence, which of course reduced the timescale of delivering the investment but also, perceived wisdom would suggest, greatly increased the risk of something going wrong. Barry and Mike relied heavily on their natural intuition and experience, which certainly worked in these cases, but was to prove fallible in some future investments, leading eventually to a need for stronger diligence, particularly as the circle of Archangel investors expanded.

Two other very important recruits to Archangels came

on board around this time. Brian Souter and his sister Ann Gloag, the founders of Stagecoach, had invited Barry to join their board and, in turn, Barry described to them what he and Mike were doing in early-stage investing. Both Brian and Ann quickly became huge supporters, both morally and financially. Both were very busy people and would not normally have been able to find the time to source, negotiate and finalise investments and so the ability to leave this to Barry and Mike, whom they trusted implicitly, was an essential ingredient of their membership of Archangels and further proof of the efficacy of a syndicate approach to angel investing.

By 1994 it was becoming apparent that the flow of investment opportunities was increasing, as were the demands of monitoring a burgeoning portfolio and an increasing number of investment partners. It was clear that the group needed some help and, by a serendipitous stroke of good fortune, Barry was introduced to Juliette Chapman, who had just moved to Edinburgh and was looking for something interesting to do.

Juliette was a smart and vivacious 30 year old who had followed a career in banking and corporate acquisition work with American Express in Paris and Credit Lyonnais in London before returning once again to Paris and thence to Edinburgh, the home town of her husband. She freely acknowledged that her career path had been somewhat unconventional and she found it difficult to find the right kind of opportunity in Edinburgh despite its renown as a financial centre.

Her meeting with Barry and Mike was, however, one that sparked mutual admiration. Juliette had become interested in the issues facing small businesses but had little practical experience of that end of the corporate market. For six months she shadowed Mike and Barry at their weekly meetings and their sessions with potential investees and very soon became an invaluable member of the team.

This introduction of an executive member of the team as 'gatekeeper' was to prove an astute and prescient move for Barry and Mike as the first inklings began to dawn that they were actually building a sustainable organisation, that is, an angel syndicate. It was unlikely that Barry and Mike and a few friends acting together in a very informal manner would be able to build much beyond what they had already done. Sifting business proposals, negotiating deals, managing existing investments and looking after investing partners are all time-consuming matters and proper executive help was required.

This is a common problem with the creation of business angel syndicates, but the appointment of executive support also brings with it a cost that somehow needs to be funded and this sometimes a problem not easy to answer. Initially, in Archangels, the cost was simply funded from the pockets of Barry and Mike, but, in time, that would also prove unfair and unsustainable and more reasonable solutions would be sought.

Meanwhile, Juliette, "our Queen bee," as Mike would call her, got down to work. There was no real precedent for her job anywhere in the world and no real job description, which was one of the reasons she enjoyed it. And so, once again, they made it up as they went along.

Juliette was primarily responsible for sifting through business proposals, which were arriving thick and fast as Barry and Mike's reputation began to grow. There were probably around 100 such proposals a year and, typically, Juliette would recommend no more than 5% of those to Barry and Mike. But the other 95% deserved to be treated seriously and the promoters encouraged or advised them as to why they might not be relevant and what they might do next. This again was to be a prime concern to Archangels: they would offer help and advice freely, even if the proposal was one that did not interest them.

"We wanted to be a roadway through, not a dead end," said Mike.

However, the criteria for making an investment decision remained somewhat haphazard. The team worked well together and had a lot of fun, although Juliette could sometimes become frustrated by the sometimes cavalier attitude to decision-making of Barry and Mike (on one occasion they declined to invest in a venture based solely on the fact that the entrepreneur in question wore a pair of white sport socks to the pitch).

"We did have a lot of laughs. You had to be light-hearted about it because there were some pretty stupid proposals," said Sandy.

But there was also some very good stuff and the trio of Barry, Mike and Sir Gerald, alongside Juliette, were moving up the learning curve of what made a sensible and ultimately profitable investment.

"In hindsight, we backed companies for different reasons: sometimes for the idea; sometimes for the potential and regularly for the people," said Juliette. "To this day, getting the combination right of the business and the people is what matters. We hadn't really got that figured out during my time."

Gradually, a broad set of rules began to emerge, many of which survive to this day. One key rule is based on geography. It is now an accepted fact that business angels tend to invest fairly locally, partly because they understand the culture, but also because if things begin to go wrong, they can act quickly and efficiently. The 'light bulb' moment for Barry, Mike and Sir Gerald came in early 1995 when they were persuaded, along with Richard Bailey, a friend of Mike's, to invest some £250,000 in the South Wales Anthracite Mining Company, which owned and operated two anthracite mines in Ammanford, South Wales.

From an early stage it became apparent that not only was hefty investment required in these former National Coal Board drift mines, but also that the prevailing culture of the management was one of exploitation of the NCB, and that continued with the new owners, clearly fuelled by a lack of documentation on coal shipments. The investors pulled out in 1996 in exasperation, licking their wounds. Mike still has a lump of Welsh anthracite on his office mantelpiece to remind him of their disastrous foray south.

This event gave rise to the first Archangel rule: *Don't make an investment unless it is within one and a half hour's drive of Edinburgh.*

"This means that, if there's a problem, as inevitably there will be, you can visit the company, try to fix it, and be back for lunch!" said Mike.

It was also in 1995 that Archangels got its name. There is some debate as to whether it was Sandy or Juliette who actually first suggested 'Archangels', but it was the natural outcome of realising that Barry and Mike were indeed business angels and then finding the name for the top echelon of angels, which they all decided had to be archangels. It was realised subsequently that seraphims and cherubims actually outrank archangels, but Mike struggled with the idea of referring to Barry as a cherub and therefore Archangels remained the chosen name.

The name was expanded to 'Archangel Informal Investment' and incorporated as a company limited by guarantee at a later stage. The word 'informal' was carefully chosen to demonstrate not just its style of engagement, but also the fact that it was an unregulated body in terms of the existing financial regulations. In fact, those regulations were quite harsh in the early years and, taken strictly, it was an offence to even pass round a business plan if there was any suggestion that investment was being sought.

"We used to break the law and get tax relief for doing it!" said Mike.

That position would change with the passing of the Financial Services and Markets Act 2000, which would allow investment opportunities to be passed to investors certified as either 'high net worth' or 'sophisticated'. But in those early days Archangels had to be very careful not to be seen to be giving advice. This was an absurd situation and one that Sandy, among others, was keen to change and lobbied the government hard to effect the change, finally brought about in 2000.

However, it was clear that the government and others were beginning to take notice of the growing importance of business angel investing and, in 1994, introduced the Enterprise Investment Scheme (EIS) as a helpful replacement for the Business Expansion Scheme. EIS remains a powerful incentive to invest in young companies, giving investors front-end tax allowances and sheltering future profits from capital gains. It recognised the high risks involved in early-stage investment while also accepting the real need for this kind of investment for the future benefit of the economy. However, Archangels and others, while applauding this initiative, were also keen to ensure that investments were made for the right commercial reasons and not solely for tax purposes. This is now generally acknowledged throughout the sector and the EIS scheme continues to be a great success.

One consequence of the rules governing EIS was that, to qualify for the tax reliefs, investors were required to invest on the same terms as other shareholders – that is, there should be no share preferences, which were, and are, rife in the professional world of venture capitalists and were proving to be a barrier to some companies seeking investment. Barry and Mike were already ahead of the game on that front, having always insisted that any investment they made would be on the same terms as the founders of the company and that they would stand 'shoulder to shoulder' on any dividend or exit rights. So EIS was right up their street.

In the previous year, there had also been recognition in Scotland of the importance of business angels, with the launch out of Glasgow Opportunities of LINC Scotland, headed by David Grahame. This was to prove an enormously helpful step, but in its initial years it was principally aimed at bringing together individual angels and companies seeking investment in a sort of 'marriage bureau' approach. Nevertheless, it did this successfully and began to grow a much higher level of interest and awareness in the concept of the business angel. In later years, LINC Scotland would become pivotal in the development of the angel sector and, in particular, the growth of other angel syndicates, which has been the real strength of the Scottish story.

Meanwhile, Archangels ploughed on with investments into a rich assortment of companies. Some of these would prove to be terrific winners but many would fall by the wayside. Whatever the result, many budding Scottish entrepreneurs would be given the opportunity to reach for the stars thanks to the financial and business guidance backing of Archangels.

From the investor perspective, failures were considered to be inevitable given the high-risk element of backing ideas and, in many cases, untried people. It was necessary to kiss a lot of frogs before finally finding a few princes, but every failure hurt and, in particular, Juliette found that difficult.

"I found it massively stressful," she said. "I should not have taken it all so personally. For Barry and Mike, with their vast experience, it was a numbers game because actually you have no idea which ones are going to work out. I blamed myself every time something went wrong. But you win one and lose ten; that was the way it was working."

It is also worth noting that the level of diligence applied to the investment decisions at this time was very light and quite substantial sums of money might be invested on the basis of intuition and judgement and even sometimes in a more social, softer sense rather than as a hard-headed business investment.

However, one investment that proved particularly disastrous, particularly quickly, also led to a fourth member joining the core group: Eric Young. Eric, a successful and well-respected businessman, had started up Eric Young & Co in 1983 as a retail property company working across the UK. He first met Mike in the early days of Stuart Wyse Ogilvie and they became firm friends, working together on a variety of property deals.

Eric was somewhat cynical about Mike's business angel investments and used to pull his leg by saying, "You're not really working this afternoon, you're just doing that Arch-angel charity stuff." Mike was determined that Eric should be involved and finally, in September 1998, he thought he had found the perfect opportunity. Barry and Mike had invested in a company called Libris Computing which had created search-engine software for library systems and was working in the National Library of Congress, the British library, NATO and the United Nations. Libris now needed a further £250,000 and Mike, having described the opportunity as a slam-dunk, persuaded Eric to invest £25,000 in that round.

Disastrously, within a week of the money being invested, a major fraud was uncovered and the company went bust. Eric was incandescent with rage and berated Mike at length on the telephone. Mike held the telephone away from his ear and eventually, when Eric had finally drawn breath, said, "For heaven's sake, Eric, where's your sense of humour!" It is a tribute to their friendship and mutual admiration that Eric not only eventually calmed down but also agreed to become the fourth core member of the group.

In 1992 only two investments were completed, the highly successful (eventually) Optos and the somewhat less successful Electronic Book Factory, which went into liquidation in March 1995. In 1993, again only two investments were made: OST and Solcom. With the addition of Juliette to the team, the pace began to pick up and the volume of investments began to rise.

In 1994 there were four new investments: Key Radio Systems, KikaFlik, Neatwork and Replyline. The first three of these did not last longer than the end of the decade and ended in liquidation, but much effort (and further investment) was put into Replyline, which flourished for a while but eventually failed in 2002.

KikaFlik is a good example of the softer approach sometimes taken by Barry and Mike in those early days. The product was a toy designed by a former nurse and gymnastic coach, Elisabeth Robertson, to encourage children and young people with hand-to-eye co-ordination. It won a number of awards, was praised by the media and even had some sales success in Hamleys and Harrods, but it was unlikely ever to be a global, let alone national, winner and eventually it was wound up in December 1995. The educational toy industry is a fiercely competitive sector and it is hardly surprising that a single product, without massive marketing spend, could fail to gain sufficient traction in that market.

Neatwork Bicycles was a cottage industry and lifestyle company based in Coldstream. Its founder, Graham Bell, approached Barry and Mike through Juliette for working capital funding to expand the business. It eventually failed in 1997, much to the disappointment of Graham, who believed that Archangels might have added more management help than it did – although it was also likely that the company was somewhat ahead of its time in terms of market demand.

Graham Bell's point about management help is interesting. Barry and Mike have always prided themselves on supplying 'smart money', which meant providing experience and help as well as cash. As the portfolio began to grow, it was becoming clear that they couldn't always be as close to their businesses as they might wish and this would need to change in future years if the success rate was to improve. In some cases, of course, they were very close to the businesses and, by and large, it was those businesses that succeeded. This realisation led to another leg being added to the organisation, with the development of a network of experienced business people, who might or might not be investors, to chair or act as non-executive advisers to the companies.

In the period 1995 to 1998 there were a further 17 new investments, many of which were to fail, but one of which, Data Discoveries, in 1995, was to be a star. Another investment in that period, Oregon Timber Frame, in 1998, remains in the Archangel portfolio and is a highly successful business continuing to provide dividend income to its shareholders and much-needed employment in the Borders of Scotland.

There were also some companies from this period that, although they never realised their full early promise, remain in business, but were either given back to their founders or sold back for very modest returns since they were clearly 'lifestyle' businesses that would not benefit from the Archangels' 'added value'.

One such business was Makar Productions, run by Eddie Dick, who had successfully run the film development and production side of Scottish Screen for some years. Makar eventually produced a film and the investors were all invited to the premiere, where Sir Gerald Elliot was heard to murmur, "This is the most expensive cinema ticket I have ever bought!" Eventually, the shares were handed back to Eddie for £1 and the investors effectively lost their money.

Data Discoveries was a good example of getting both the management team and the product right. The founder, Marcus Brook, was introduced to Archangels by Alison Loudon, who was chairing Replyline, and an investment was agreed in October 1995. Alison also introduced David Aitken as technical director. David had been a colleague of Ian Ritchie, the founder of Office Workstations, which had developed a hypertext web browser that was sold to Panasonic in 1989 for £8 million.

Marcus and David began developing specialised software for data capture, database cleaning and debtor tracing, but it soon became clear that the team needed to be strengthened by a top-class sales supremo and Mike persuaded a friend of his, Gordon Galloway, to take on the short-term task of building a sales force.

That 'short-term task' turned into a ten-year stretch, with Gordon taking over the reins as managing director and skilfully guiding the company to great success. In 1999 it won the Deloitte & Touche Technology Fast 50 Scotland award and the following year it won the prestigious UK award in the Deloitte Fast Track 50, recording an astonishing sales growth of 9,307% in just three years.

Data Discoveries began to develop sustainable profitability and was able to pay significant dividends to its shareholders before being successfully sold in 2011, making substantial gains for its management team and the Archangels investors. Barry made 5.45 times his original investment.

But in 1998 the Archangels investors made their first really successful exit. Objective Software Technologies was sold in January 1998 at a price that made a return for Barry, Mike and Sir Gerald of more than 1,000%. It also turned its founders into millionaires overnight. So the first real return from any of the investments was hugely successful and gave encouragement for the future, despite the many losses incurred on the way.

By 1999, changes were afoot. Juliette had decided that she wanted to reduce her commitment. Nelson Gray, who had invested alongside Barry and Mike in several companies and who had been helping Juliette in some of the investment appraisal, agreed to take on more of a lead role. But Nelson was also involved in a number of other activities, such as East of Scotland Investment, and found it difficult to give enough time to the job.

In addition, despite the success of OST, there had been many failures and even those investments that showed some promise needed extra rounds of funding, which were beginning to stretch the pockets of the individual investors.

These factors were clearly evident in the reduction of new company investment activity. In 1999 only one new investment was made, into a company called Gencell. However, in some respects the timing of all this was perfect since it meant that there were low levels of activity just as the infamous dotcom boom was starting, which Archangels therefore avoided – meaning it also (largely) avoided the spectacular dotcom bust.

To be fair, one investment sale was made in late 1999, Solcom Systems, but this was a paper exchange for shares quoted on NASDAQ, which were not readily cashable in the short term and, frankly, at that early stage were not hugely valuable – although, as we have seen, this was to change dramatically.

But Barry, Mike, Sir Gerald and Eric were keen to find a way to continue and, in early 2000, persuaded Peter Shakeshaft to take on the role of gatekeeper.

In the eight years from 1992 to 1999 inclusive, Archangels invested in 26 companies. Of these, 16 (61.5%) failed completely and provided no return to the investors; six (23%) were eventually sold successfully; three (11.5%) were effectively handed back to their founders for no gain or loss, and one company (4%) remained in the portfolio. Seventeen of the 26 companies needed more than one round of investment and the period from first investment to successful sale took between five and 16 years.

From Barry's records (excluding Optos), he made gains from the successful sales of companies of £1,187,000, suffered losses from those that failed of £670,000 and therefore made an overall gain of £517,000. Mike's record is similar, given that they both invested in equal proportions over the years. The returns from successful exits varied between 210% to over 1,000% and, even given the opportunity cost of money during the period, represented a remarkable return.

It is also worth recording that when Optos eventually

floated, Barry sold 15% of his shareholding, which covered all of his cost of investment to that date, which implies, depending on share price movements, a return of at least 600% on his investment.

So, despite all the failures, these early years had proved profitable to Archangels and, more than that, had given many people an ability to explore their ideas; had created new entrepreneurs; had provided employment in Scotland; and had encouraged innovation in a number of sectors. Barry and Mike's vision was beginning to have a real effect on the economic landscape of Scotland.

3

EVOLUTION NOT REVOLUTION

The start of the new century in 2000 was to herald a period of evolution for Archangels that would see it recognised in Scotland as a serious force for good in the area of young company investment and innovation. The next six years would bring a number of key changes that would prove the sustainability of the syndicate and extend the concept of angel investment to become a vital part of the Scottish young company environment.

In February 2000, Peter Shakeshaft was appointed as the new gatekeeper of Archangels. In stark contrast to the youthful Juliette, Peter was a battle-scarred business veteran in his 50s, but he was to become a gentle catalyst for change at Archangels, bringing it a sense of order and direction.

Born in 1947, Peter lived his early life in Glasgow and qualified as a chartered accountant in 1970. Immediately after qualifying, he entered industry and held a number of senior financial positions until in 1980 he became chairman and chief executive of a printing group, which he ran successfully and sold to John Waddington in 1987. He was a director of Waddingtons in Yorkshire for three years but hankered to get back to Scotland and so he returned, this time to Edinburgh, in 1990 to take up the role of chief executive of the Drambuie Group. Following this he decided to start up his own business and bought a knitwear company with the idea of creating a high-quality group of Scottish companies along the lines of LVMH. Sadly, this did not work out and Peter, for the first time in his career, tasted failure. However, he then carried out the turnaround of a substantial company and, in 1996, decided to take on a number of non-executive roles for 3i and others.

It was at this time that he was introduced to Barry through Ewan Brown of Noble Grossart, whom Peter had introduced as a non-executive director in his printing group. Barry asked Peter to chair a couple of his pre-Archangels companies: Interface Graphics, which Peter subsequently sold successfully, and Addabox. At a later stage, Peter was also asked to chair Replyline, an Archangels investment.

In 1999, for personal reasons, Peter gave up all his non-executive work, including three companies he chaired for 3i, and effectively spent six months doing not very much. But by early 2000, he was ready for another challenge and spoke with Barry to get some ideas. This is when Barry persuaded him to take on the gatekeeper role at Archangels.

"This was the best job in Scotland," said Peter Shakeshaft.

"I know that for a fact because Barry told me that when he was trying to persuade me to take it on."

In fact, Peter took little persuasion. At that stage it looked as if it was a job that he could do for a couple of days a week, largely from his home in East Lothian, and it suited his purposes admirably. Eventually, of course, it turned into eight days a week, but that was some way down the line.

Although Peter was clearly an experienced businessman and was well versed in the buying and selling of companies, he had little experience of investing in young businesses and his first year at Archangels was something of a baptism of fire.

To begin with, he simply picked up where Juliette had left off. There were several deals in the pipeline that had been agreed in principle and which he took through to completion working with Stuart Hendry, Sandy's associate, with whom Peter was to work closely over the next six years. He also started to review the incoming business plans, rejecting many at the first pass but taking some forward to the investors for further appraisal. There were no real guidelines and much was done by instinct and feel. In fact, the first new deal for which Peter received approval was an absolute disaster, which Barry and Mike have never let him forget.

The Flower Company was a fledgling business based in Midlothian that specialised in hand-arranging and dispatching bespoke flower arrangements nationwide. It was a cottage industry business run by an ambitious owner who believed that, with proper funding, she could build a much larger and more viable business. Peter brought it to the attention of Barry, Mike, Sir Gerald and Eric, who were clearly not very impressed but agreed that Peter should take it forward and they invested £75,000 in May 2000. Predictably (with hindsight) it failed fairly quickly and was liquidated in August 2001. This was an object lesson for Peter, although he believes that the guys had a pretty good idea it would fail and wanted to ensure he went through that experience. Certainly it was a lesson on how an investment can go wrong quickly.

In fact, Peter's first year as gatekeeper of Archangels was not marked by great success. The syndicate invested in nine new companies, of which eight were later to fail and only one saw success with flotation in 2006. Not an auspicious start, but Peter was beginning to focus on the process and infrastructure of the syndicate, recognising that there were some inherent weaknesses alongside the undoubted flair and intuition of the key members. The key was to somehow fix the weaknesses without losing the flair and informality that marked out the true angel approach.

There was also a growing realisation that the companies in the portfolio needed further rounds of funding if they were to achieve their goals and that the perceived natural handover to venture capitalists was not going to work. Indeed, in 2000, Archangels pumped in a further £900,000 to Optos, which was beginning to find market traction but also needed significant funding as it grew. This lack of an ability to build relationships with VCs was a sore that would run for many years and had, at its core, the difference between the angel structure of funding, which rested on equality with the founders, versus an aggressive but understandable requirement of the VCs to take preferences on exits.

It was becoming abundantly clear that, as levels of activity grew and more people became involved, the emerging syndicate needed to become more organised and transparent in its dealings. In July 2000, Archangels was formed into a company limited by guarantee (that is, one that could not distribute its profits) and the first directors were Barry, Mike, Sir Gerald and Eric. By popular acclaim, Mike was appointed as the chairman of the company. This structure allowed Peter to insist on formal monthly board meetings, not only to review potential investments, but also to monitor the performance of all of the companies in the portfolio.

This board became known as the 'core' of Archangels and all other members became known as the 'outer circle'. Indeed, there was a growing number of other members (approximately 50 at this stage) and there was a need to interact with them, both professionally and fairly. The introduction of the Financial Services and Markets Act 2000 gave significantly more freedom to Archangels to deal with their wider circle of members and, provided that such members were able to be certified as 'high net worth' individuals or 'sophisticated investors', then opportunities to invest could be given to them, although strictly no advice could be proffered.

However, there was a further problem: some of the members were a little suspicious that Barry and Mike would pass on investment opportunities only where the risk was particularly high and would keep the best ones to themselves. This was, of course, scurrilous nonsense, but a way had to be found to scotch the perception. Thus was born the new and unbreakable rule that *any new investment decision or refunding decision had to be the unanimous decision of the board of Archangels and that each board member would commit £20,000 of his own money to the investment and the remainder would be offered out to the outer circle.* Board members could invest more than their £20,000 but only in parallel with the offer to the outer circle. These rules allowed transparency in how the board dealt with the outer circle and also gave them comfort that each investment had passed the test of all board members and that all board members were actually putting their money where their mouth was.

There remained the question of how the costs of the syndicate would be covered, which largely consisted of remuneration for the gatekeeper and other staff who would join later. Each member of the board agreed to pay £5,000 towards such costs and both Brian Souter and Ann Gloag, although not board members, agreed to do the same. There was no membership fee or subscription charged to the outer circle members, but, if any individual member decided to invest, then he or she was charged an administration fee of 5% of their investment. A further decision was made that no fee would be charged to the investee company at the time of investment, which was a reflection of the directors' firm view that profit should be made from the investment and not the process. However, it was decided to introduce a modest annual monitoring fee for each investment to enable central costs of that process to be covered.

Some structure was therefore being put in place, but none of it interfered with the flair for decision-making or the speed at which transactions could be completed.

One further innovation was introduced at the end of 2000: Archangels issued its first ever press release summarising its activities for the year. The principal reason for this was to make budding entrepreneurs aware that there was still at least one source of funding available to them if they had a good plan. The dotcom bust was beginning to have a devastating effect on capital available from venture capitalists, most of whom had put up the shutters to early-stage investment and some of whom had already left Scotland. Archangels needed to encourage the continuation of entrepreneurialism in Scotland and to some extent was filling the vacuum left by the fleeing VCs.

Extracts from that first press release put out on 9 January 2001 read:

> "The Scottish based Archangel Informal Investment, the business angel group, completed a record year for investment in fledgling and start-up companies in 2000. Members of the Archangel syndicate personally invested £3.3m during the year in private companies and attracted further funding to those companies of £4.6m from banks and institutions."

Mike Rutterford wrote:

"This has been an exciting year for Archangels, reflecting the confidence and exuberance of the business start-up sector in Scotland. We have been around for a long time as business angels and we are used to high risk/high reward investments, but the quality of the proposals has significantly improved, giving us renewed confidence to invest. We are keen to help companies not just with money, but also by bringing our experience to bear to help them through the tough times."

Shortly after this press release, a meeting was held with all members of the syndicate to discuss the activities during the year and to look forward to the following year. This meeting was to become an important annual event, comprising investee companies and the investors and became known as the 'Archangels chorus'.

The next couple of years would build on the foundations laid down in 2000. The criteria for investment became clearer and, although failure in some investments was inevitable, given the high-risk status of early-stage investing, the success rate gradually began to improve. Archangels was also prepared to commit to bigger front-end investment, given the growing number of members and, in December 2001, completed its biggest deal to date by investing £2 million in CXR Biosciences, a spin-out from Dundee University.

But this was no ordinary spin-out. Normally a university spin-out would comprise the commercialisation of an early-stage idea protected by patent and might involve the hiring of one, perhaps two, part-time university staff who had created the idea. CXR involved the transfer of the whole department of Xenomics (short for Xenopus genomics – the marriage of Xenopus as a model organism for cell and development biology with genomic approaches) out of Dundee University under the leadership of Professor Roland Wolf and a significant array of intellectual property.

Mike and Roland had met at a dinner party hosted by Douglas Anderson (of Optos fame) and Mike had been hugely impressed with Roland, who was also honorary director of Cancer Research UK Molecular Pharmacology Unit and was deeply interested in understanding the pathways that determine the sensitivity of human cells to drugs, agents and toxins. By complete chance, Barry and Mike met Roland at Newark airport in 2000 and discussions began as to how Roland's work might be spun out of Dundee University and properly commercialised. When Barry and Mike returned to the UK, they asked Peter to start discussions with Roland and the university, but it was to take fully 18 months of hard negotiation before, on Christmas Eve 2001, the deal was finally completed and CXR Biosciences was born.

There were four other new investments in 2001, two of which – Hanon Solutions, which was sold at a loss, and White Dentalcare – would eventually fail. One of the others, Arrayjet, remains in the Archangel portfolio and the fourth, Gyneideas, was sold successfully in 2010, yielding a return for the original investors of 220% and an even higher return for some of the later investors.

A further significant step in the enhancement of the reputation of Archangels came with the addition as a board member of Gavin Gemmell, who became the fifth core member of the syndicate. Gavin was a hugely respected figure in financial circles. Born and educated in Edinburgh and qualifying as a chartered accountant, Gavin joined Baillie Gifford as an investment trainee in 1964 and became a partner in 1967. He was senior partner for 15 years before retiring in 2001; he oversaw an expansion of the business from 35 staff with £350 million under management to an astonishing 400 staff with £22 billion under management when he retired. Baillie Gifford has continued to be highly successful and currently employs over 900 people and manages over £100 billion. He also became a non-executive director of Scottish Widows in 1984 and was appointed chairman in 2002, which also brought with it membership of the parent group board, Lloyds TSB. His agreement to join the Archangels board was indeed a powerful acknowledgement of the importance of the syndicate in Scotland.

Progress was also being made on the need to build a proper infrastructure for Archangels. The days when Peter could operate two days a week from his home in East Lothian were long gone and Mike generously found a couple of attic rooms in his office at 111 George Street that, for a time, became the home of Archangels and were furnished lavishly with a couple of trestle tables and four tubular steel school chairs.

Nevertheless, it did the job and Peter used the opportunity when interviewing young hopeful entrepreneurs to point out what starting a business in a garret was really like. However, soon after this, Mike bought a couple of buildings in Rutland Square and the ground floor of number 20 Rutland Square became the proper headquarters of Archangels, where it remains. This time the offices were fitted out beautifully with the soft furnishings being chosen by Mike's wife June and a boardroom table and 12 chairs being bought from a friend of Mike's for the princely sum of £500.

But there was also a need for more people to cope with the fast-growing needs of the organisation. The next key person to join Peter was Robert Pattullo, who had been one of the original investors in Optos and who had worked closely with Barry at Christian Salvesen. However, after leaving Salvesen, Robert had worked with Nelson Gray at Gap Fund Managers and had gained a huge understanding of the special needs of young companies. When Robert joined Archangels, Peter was juggling the requirements of reviewing some 200 business plans a year while still having to monitor the performance and needs of the growing portfolio of investments. Robert's arrival allowed Peter to pass over responsibility for the portfolio and Robert soon began to compile an excellent matrix of portfolio company performance, which allowed the directors to properly review, on a monthly basis, the status and requirements of all the investments.

The final, and much-needed, member of the team came with the appointment of Peter's daughter, Katie, as secretary. Katie had worked as a legal secretary for one of the top legal firms in Edinburgh, but, in true entrepreneurial style, had left that firm to set up her own business offering part-time secretarial services to a growing band of self-employed individuals who needed some help with their administration. Peter persuaded Katie to join Archangels on a part-time client basis, which soon turned into a full-time position that would last until 2008.

This trio, based at 20 Rutland Square, would effectively run Archangels for the next four years, carrying out the review of 200 business plans a year, making around 20 new and refunding investments in each year, monitoring a portfolio of 30–40 investee companies, managing an outer circle membership of 50–80 individuals, building a network of potential non-executive directors and chairmen and, most difficult of all, satisfying the board of Archangels with its diverse requirements. It was hard work but it was also great fun.

Fortuitously, it was also at this time that Archangels formed a closer relationship with LINC Scotland, led by David Grahame. LINC Scotland's relevance to the development of Archangels, at this stage, was its ability to find a method of funding for the growing central costs of the syndicate, which helped enormously during this period and, without which, it might have proved impossible to bring sufficient resources to bear to continue the growth.

David Grahame, through his creation and then leadership of LINC Scotland, has probably done more than any other to build Scotland's prime position as a nation of business angels. Born in Hawick, David graduated from St Andrews University and went into the hospitality industry, first opening a restaurant in Cupar in Fife and then another, the Grange, also in Fife. However, his timing was not perfect and the fall-off of overseas visitors in the late 80s caused David to sell up and enter a more conventional career with Glasgow's Enterprise Trust, where he became head of business development.

It was during his time with the Enterprise Trust, Glasgow Opportunities, that David became aware of the potential growth of business angels as a source of finance and advice for young companies. In 1993, LINC Scotland was spun out of Glasgow Opportunities, under the directorship of David, and he began to concentrate solely on the business angel market.

Uniquely, LINC Scotland was classified as an enterprise agency in its own right, which brought with it tax advantages, exemption from the financial services regulations and an ability to apply to Europe for funding. These were powerful tools to add effectiveness in the drive to build a business angel community in Scotland.

To begin with, LINC concentrated its efforts on educating and attracting potential business angels and creating a kind of marriage bureau service to match young companies seeking finance with these business angels. But there was a growing awareness that the most effective way forward for sustainable angel investing was by forming syndicates. In 2001 David developed a mechanism to help fund the inevitable central costs of angel syndicates and Archangels became the first to benefit, thereby starting a long and mutually beneficial relationship between Archangels and LINC.

David and LINC were pivotal in influencing the introduction of the Scottish Co-investment Fund to include angel syndicates and, from that point on, were instrumental in encouraging new syndicates to be formed. In 2001 there were only two syndicates in Scotland. There are now 19, the vast majority of which were assisted by LINC. New syndicates are being formed at the rate of two or three a year and this is seen as a necessary growth rate as the more mature syndicates become responsible for the ongoing funding of their existing, growing portfolios.

David also formed a group called the Angel Leaders Forum, which brought these syndicates together to discuss areas of common concern (and occasionally to do deals together, which lent even more strength to the marketplace).

Eventually, LINC broke free of its association with Glasgow Opportunities and became owned by its membership, giving it a truly pan-Scotland dimension. Peter Shakeshaft became chairman in 2007 through to 2013, during which time LINC became a sustainable, although still a not-for-profit, organisation. It is seen as the prime partner of Scottish Enterprise in the support of business angels, the leading adviser to both Scottish and Westminster government (including the Treasury) on angel matters and is frequently visited by overseas countries seeking to learn how to develop business angels in their homelands.

By 2002 it was clear that the funding environment for early-stage companies in Scotland was becoming very difficult. The venture capitalists had all but disappeared and the banks were beginning to take a jaundiced view of the sector, with the result that business angels were pretty well the only game in town. However, the need for Archangels to continue funding existing portfolio companies was becoming quite a strain and having an inevitable impact on its ability to fund new ideas. Indeed, in 2002, Archangels members invested some £1.5 million in new companies, but £4.3 million in its existing portfolio. In his review of that year, Peter wrote:

> *"By any yardstick, 2002 was a difficult year for start-up and early stage companies, both in terms of raising finance and achieving business goals. The increase in proposals received is indicative of the drop in active funders in the marketplace and of the rising profile of Archangels. The proposals generally were of better quality and greater realism in terms of the amount of funding being sought. There was also a high proportion of proposals from companies previously funded elsewhere but which could not attract further funding from existing shareholders."*

This vital funding gap for new businesses was recognised by the Scottish government and discussions began to take place as to how it might be resolved. These discussions would eventually lead to the creation of the Scottish Co-investment Fund (SCIF) in 2003, one of the most imaginative and effective interventions that any government has ever undertaken. The SCIF created a sea change in young company investment in Scotland at a very important tipping point in funding availability. Effectively, after its launch, partner angel syndicates, such as Archangels, could draw down up to 100% matching funds for any investment they undertook, thereby doubling the fire power of the syndicate at a single stroke. Given the increasing strain on the pockets of the business angels, this was a huge fillip for the funding of early-stage companies in Scotland.

Without doubt, the most important support mechanism for business angel syndicates in Scotland was the launch of SCIF. This was an imaginative and unique initiative designed to support equity investment into young companies alongside private investors. But it very nearly didn't happen and there were many twists and turns before it finally emerged.

In the late 90s, Scottish Enterprise (SE) decided that there was little evidence that further support was needed in terms of equity backing of Scottish companies and in early 2000 it spun off the highly successful Scottish Development Finance to form a new private stand-alone organisation, Scottish Equity Partners (SEP). SEP was to act as a full-blown venture capital house under its directors, Calum Paterson and Brian Kerr, who had managed Scottish Development Finance. Its focus changed away from purely Scottish companies to cover the whole of the UK and Ireland and, therefore, a major player in the Scottish market was virtually lost overnight.

With hindsight, this was not a well-timed move since during 2000–2001 it became apparent to SE that there was, once again, a significant gap appearing in the equity market, particularly for SMEs in the sub-£1 million range. The dotcom bust was underway and the conventional venture capitalists had fled the scene. The business angel sector was just about the only game in town, but angel syndicates were being stretched to look after their own portfolios, and funding for new businesses was becoming tight. SE decided that some form of intervention was again needed to stimulate the market.

The initial concept was to put together a fund comprising central government money, private money and European money from the European Regional Development Fund (ERDF). However, this concept never really got off the ground since private investors would not invest in a fund for which they would get no EIS relief, nor would they sit behind public investment decisions.

Gradually, the idea of some form of co-investment approach began to emerge. As with all these things, the real genesis for the concept is shrouded in some haziness. The first public pronouncement of the idea came from Wendy Alexander, who was Scotland's Minister for

Enterprise and Life-Long Learning and whose support was critical if the idea was to get off the ground. But it is clear that there were very high-level discussions going on at the top of SE led by its deputy chairman, Professor Neil Hood, and its chief executive, Robert Crawford. There was also consultation being held with interested parties, such as LINC and Archangels, as to how such a scheme might operate and the first moves were being made to see whether funds could be raised from the ERDF.

Things started to gather pace with the commitment by the Scottish government of £30 million to the project in the belief that a similar amount might be forthcoming from the ERDF. Gerard Kelly was put in charge of the project within SE, ably assisted by Pat McHugh, a European expert, and Martin Hughes, an economist.

The application to Europe for ERDF funds was an enormous task. This was an entirely new concept for the European Commission and it went right to the top of the Commission for a decision. There was some disquiet that it might breach state aid regulations or fall foul of Europe's powerful competition laws. It was touch and go, and the SE team spent many hours going round the houses in Brussels explaining the concept and answering the myriad concerns.

But while all that was going on, another major stumbling block was looming. It became clear to David Grahame of LINC that the fund rules were being drawn up on the basis of co-investing with VCs only and not business angels, which was entirely counter-intuitive to what was really happening in the marketplace. Not only were VCs inactive in the marketplace, they didn't really need additional funds from SE. Something had to be done, and done quickly, to change SE's mind before an announcement was made.

A meeting was arranged on 25 June 2002 with Robert Crawford at the Glasgow office of Biggart Baillie attended by David Grahame, Peter Shakeshaft and three or four others. David put up a slide showing the investment activity of venture capitalists in Scotland over the past two years compared to that of business angels and the figures were stark. Peter recalls that Robert's jaw dropped and he twigged the problem straight away. To his credit, Robert immediately agreed that something would have to be done, but there was a further problem. By their very nature, business angels fell outwith the financial regulations and, therefore, Robert faced the unenviable task of finding a way to commit public money alongside unregulated investors. No easy task, but Peter Shakeshaft was blunt: "Unless you find a way, this fund will fail and you are not going to get the money directed to where it should go," he said. According to legend, Robert Crawford returned to his headquarters in Bothwell Street and immediately convened a meeting of the project team to find an answer, which, to its eternal credit, it duly did.

"The fund was a huge leap of imagination for a public sector economic development agency," said David Grahame. "This was uncharted territory in saying that they would join together with unregulated investors from the private sector. To their great credit, they didn't shirk from it and worked hard to put in place a workable solution."

Robert Crawford said, "I have no doubt that Peter Shakeshaft and David Grahame were great lobbyists and massively helpful too. SCIF has been a terrific and much copied initiative and I'm very proud of it."

And so the fund was finally launched on 31 March 2003 with European funds being committed shortly thereafter. Of course there were rules attached to the European funds, but these were all managed by SE and the first two partners, Archangels and Braveheart, were appointed with the first deal being done soon thereafter by Archangels.

It is perhaps worthwhile dwelling a little on how the fund works and what made it unique at the time. Key to the process is the appointment of partners and the contract between the partners and SCIF. Peter Shakeshaft was again responsible for the final negotiations on the terms of that contract, which allow a partner to apply, under certain simple rules, for a matching investment by SCIF of up to £500,000 into any one company in which the partner itself is investing. SCIF performs diligence in the first instance on the partners before they are appointed but undergoes no further diligence on the investee company and invests under the same terms as the partner. Thus, the process is efficient and quick and an approach for investment can be made only through a partner and not directly to SCIF.

SCIF is now run under the auspices of The Scottish Investment Bank, a division of SE, together with two other equity funds, The Scottish Seed Fund, for funding of between £20,000 and £250,000, and the Scottish Venture Fund, for funding of between £500,000 and £2 million. Both of these latter two funds operate under different rules from SCIF but, together, the three funds provide powerful equity support for Scottish companies.

Interestingly, in an independent review of SCIF's first five years of operation it was noted that 82% of its 245 deals over that period had been initiated by business angel syndicates, thus vindicating the view that angels needed to be partners to make it work.

Another notable indication of the need for angels to replace venture capitalists came about in October 2002 with the annual Connect Investment Conference. This conference had been held in Edinburgh for a number of years and was an opportunity for young companies and entrepreneurs to pitch to an audience of venture capitalists, business angels and other funders for finance. In every previous year, the conference had been sponsored by the big venture capitalists, but in 2002 no such sponsor could be found. However, rather than see it fail, Archangels decided to step into the gap and provide the necessary sponsorship for it to take place.

Peter Shakeshaft, in his sponsorship speech to the conference dinner, said:

"I really shouldn't be here. Archangels has never sponsored anything before and is unlikely to do so again. It is not our style.

However, we are not prepared to see this great annual opportunity for entrepreneurs in Scotland to showcase their wonderful innovations and inventions fall by the wayside for want of a few pounds. Support for new companies is vital and certainly we remain open for business."

Inevitably, however, the need to continue to refinance the existing portfolio began to take a serious toll on both the financial resources of the Archangels members and the time resources of the small executive team. This is now recognised as a common problem for syndicates as they mature and is one of the reasons that the continuing creation of new syndicates, which is led in Scotland by LINC Scotland, is so important to the continuance of support for new companies.

However, Archangels still undertook some important new investments over the next few years. Among these were Gyneideas and Lab901, both of which would be sold with varying degrees of success; Stem Cell Sciences, which was briefly floated on the stock exchange but subsequently failed; and a number of others, such as Arrayjet, Lux Innovate, Reactec, Indigo Lighthouse and Document Outsourcing, which remain in the portfolio. But, of course, there were also a number of failures.

Meanwhile, there were to be further changes to the board of Archangels. In 2003, Sir Gerald Elliot retired from the board, having given huge support from the beginning, both in a financial and an advisory capacity. His sharp mind, quick wit and rapier-like questioning would be sadly missed but he continued to be supportive of the syndicate in many ways, not least financially. Sir Gerald's replacement on the board was another businessman held in the highest esteem in Scotland and internationally.

Dr Ian Sword was the chairman of Inveresk Research, which he had originally bought out from the Scottish Development Agency in 1984 and built into a highly successful drug development services company employing around 1,600 people from its base near Edinburgh. He first sold Inveresk in 1989 to Société Générale de Surveillance but bought it back some years later under a pre-emption clause and continued to grow the company. In 2002 it was listed on NASDAQ and eventually sold to Charles River Laboratories in 2004. Ian had been chairman of Scottish Enterprise Edinburgh and Lothian from which he retired in 2002, but this experience had further piqued his interest in the life science culture in Scotland and he readily accepted Barry's offer to join the board of Archangels.

Ian's first involvement with Archangels was significant and again arose from the lack of funding sources in Scotland, apart from angels, at that time. Stem Cell Sciences had originally been spun out of Edinburgh University to commercialise the world-beating technology being developed by Professor Austin Smith, who was doing pioneering work in embryonic stem cell research. The company had moved to Australia, partly for regulatory reasons, but also because that was where some investment money was to be found. It wanted to move back to

Scotland to be close to its research base but could find no backers until Archangels came on the scene.

Archangels assembled an investment package of £2.45 million, including funding from the Scottish Co-investment Fund and an Australian private equity house, and completed the investment in 2003. The company set up its headquarters in Edinburgh. It was floated on AIM and on the Australian Securities Exchange in April 2007 but eventually it flopped and the chief executive, with whom Archangels had always had an uneasy relationship, had his appointment terminated.

In many ways, Stem Cell Sciences was a good example of investing in something before its proper time.

"Commercialising stem cells remains a big hope," said Ian Sword. "It was a great opportunity for Scotland to get ahead when the United States banned research in this area. We are getting there in areas of research in Scotland. There is now a huge amount of work going on globally and it is moving in the right direction, but it is a lot slower than we thought. Unfortunately, Stem Cell Sciences wasn't successful."

Another key investment in 2003 was Touch Emas (now Touch Bionics), which was the first-ever spin-out from NHS Scotland under the newly created Scottish Health Innovation Ltd (SHIL).

The important role of universities in providing innovative ideas and candidates for commercial spin-out companies has been noted before but, in 2002, NHS Scotland also became important, through the creation of SHIL. Prior to the existence of SHIL there was no mechanism available for the National Health Service to benefit from the inventions and innovations it spawned, given its inability to hold investments for profit or deal in risk capital. Historically, any innovations emerging from NHS Scotland, and there had been many, found their way into commercial hands with no reward flowing back into the health service.

The creation of SHIL was spearheaded by Dr Alison Spaull of the Scottish government's Chief Scientist Office, who researched similar institutions worldwide and came up with the SHIL model, which effectively could hold equity stakes in companies on behalf of NHS Scotland and execute licensing deals that allowed royalty flows back to the health service. Thus the route to commercialisation was opened up to NHS Scotland in much the same way as the universities had operated for many years. It was funded by the Chief Scientist Office, Scottish Enterprise, Highland and Islands Enterprise, the UK Department for Business, Innovation and Skills and the European Regional Development Funds.

But, crucially for such a publicly funded body, its original constitution required that the majority of its directors should be drawn from the private sector and – although there was inevitably a softer side, of spreading best practice around the health boards, which were non-income-producing – it was capable of making hard-headed commercial decisions for the benefit of both the inventors and the health service.

The first chairman of SHIL was Barry Sealey, who was succeeded in 2007 by Peter Shakeshaft. Other directors included Sandy Finlayson and Colin Morgan, head of Johnson & Johnson in Scotland. SHIL has been responsible for creating a number of product licences and a number of spin-out companies, the first of which was Touch Bionics.

Touch Bionics' founder and inventor, David Gow, had developed the world's first bionic arm while working within NHS Scotland. Barry Sealey was then chairman of Edinburgh Healthcare Trust and became aware of David's work and its possible commercial application. He asked Peter to find a way to spin the company out of NHS Scotland but still leave some interest in ownership for the NHS in any resulting company. Peter spent 18 months trying to solve this problem but could find no acceptable answer as it was fundamentally against the rules of the NHS that they could hold any private interests.

However, in 2003 SHIL was established as the vehicle to investigate and commercialise opportunities arising in NHS Scotland and at last Touch Bionics could be created. The deal was that each of the parties – SHIL, David Gow, as founder, and Archangels – would own one-third of the capital of the company. Subsequently, Touch Bionics needed much more funding to develop and grow its business, which led to inevitable dilution for SHIL and David, but it is now a world leader in upper limb prostheses with sales of £15 million.

In 2016 it was sold to Össur, an Icelandic prosthetics company, for £27.5 million, providing a platform for further international growth and netting a tidy profit for the founders in the process.

The final proof of Archangels, together with other emerging angel syndicates, filling the vacuum left by the flight of the venture capitalists came in 2004 when Archangels alone invested £8.6 million in early-stage companies in Scotland compared to just £7 million from all members of the British Venture Capital Association. In that same year, Peter Shakeshaft was awarded the prestigious title of Scottish Dealmaker of the Year, an award that had in every previous year been given to a venture capitalist or a high-profile corporate lawyer.

4

THE F WORD

Why so many failures? This is a recurring question that vexes many business angel syndicates and one that, in 2004, Peter Shakeshaft was asked by the board of Archangels to analyse. It is widely accepted that angel investing is high risk/high reward and that there are bound to be failures from ideas that simply don't work or are uncommercial or, perhaps, are 'before their time'. The trick is to make lots of money from the few that are successful and lose less money from those that fail. The general rule is often quoted that from a basket of ten investments, four will fail, four will never achieve their original potential and may become zombies, and perhaps two will be shooting stars achieving significant returns. This is one of the reasons that angel syndicates are growing in popularity since they allow members to spread their risk over a bigger basket of investments than they could usually hope to achieve on their own.

However, if the number of failures could be reduced, then the returns would clearly be greater. Peter's research into the reasons for failure culminated in a list of do's and don'ts that was broadly adopted by the board:

1. *We should avoid leaps of enthusiasm before basic due diligence.*
2. *Each proposal that comes to the board should have at least one 'board champion' who has been involved in the review process.*
3. *We should make more use of external diligence facilities (using people we know and trust) and be prepared to pay for it.*
4. *Irrespective of the chairmanship or non-executive director in a company, each one of our investee companies should be allocated an Archangel board member or executive to liaise with the company on a regular basis.*
5. *We should be prepared to act more quickly if we feel there are management or non-executive weaknesses.*
6. *We should be more disciplined in applying our investment criteria of 'high growth potential' and 'global application' and avoid diversions.*
7. *We should be more aggressive at an earlier stage in pursuing exits for companies that are lagging behind expectations.*
8. *We need to improve the sales, marketing and business development skills in our investee companies at an earlier stage.*
9. *We should continue to explore potential partnerships or mechanisms to provide adequate follow-on funds.*
10. *We should consider bringing in external diligence for an independent view of any unplanned refinancings.*

It can be seen from this list that one of the most difficult areas is the decision as to whether or not investee companies deserve further unplanned funding rounds if they have failed in their first ambitions. This is a tricky subject since clearly money has already been invested and there is a fine line between throwing in the towel too early and potentially just putting in more money to protect the first tranches. Sometimes this is a difficult judgement, made even more difficult due to relationships that have been built up over the time of the investment. With hindsight, it is likely that some 'follow-on' funding should not have taken place and some companies should have been allowed to fail earlier. It is equally true that changes in senior management were made only reluctantly and could perhaps have brought benefits if actioned at an earlier stage.

Archangels liked to say that it was a 'patient investor', by which it meant to differentiate itself from the relative short-termism of the venture capitalists, but, in reality, it believed that if a good company could be built up independently, then an exit opportunity would present itself at the appropriate time. In the current climate, that philosophy for business angels has largely changed and nowadays there is usually a pre-investment discussion as to who the potential buyers of the company might be, so that the strategy of the company can be aligned to real exit opportunities.

Towards the end of Peter's tenure, activity remained at a high level. Both Peter and Robert Pattullo had joined the board of Archangels, which required Peter to give up his beloved title of gatekeeper for the more mundane but appropriate title of chief executive. In 2005 an additional director was also appointed, which broke the mould in many ways and typified Archangels' approach to Scotland. Sarah Smith was Head of Strategy and Delivery Units at the Scottish Executive and her appointment to the Archangels board on 1 January 2005 was the result of a meeting between Barry and John Elvidge, Head of the Scottish Executive.

Barry suggested to John that it would be a good idea for some of the up-and-coming members of the Scottish Executive to get some appreciation of business life by acting as non-executive directors of some of the Archangels companies. John proposed Sarah but, when Barry and Peter met with Sarah, it was strikingly obvious that her real role, both as student and teacher, should be with the main Archangels board and so she became a much valued non-executive of that board and brought a welcome fresh viewpoint to the meetings.

Aside from continuing normal investment activity, there was also growing interest in taking part in consortia that were being put together to work alongside the UK's Enterprise Capital Fund. One such consortium was later launched as Seraphim, which was an angel-led fund to which Archangels and eight other partners in England and the USA each committed £1 million, which was matched by the UK government. Peter brought in Sandy Finlayson to help pull it all together.

By the middle of 2005, Peter wanted to step back from the lead position and it was agreed that some senior help would be sought so that Peter could reduce his time commitment. With great serendipity, just at this time John Waddell, who was working at Noble Grossart and who had previously worked with Barry at Salvesen, approached Barry to say he was looking for a new challenge. Peter and the board of Archangels realised that John would be ideal for the job and indeed, so good, that it would allow Peter to step down entirely, which is what he really wanted to do.

Meanwhile, Peter, who was asked to stay on the Archangel board as a non-executive director for a couple of years, continued his interest in early-stage and emerging companies by chairing LINC Scotland and Scottish Health Innovation Ltd. His last investment for Archangels, in July 2005, was Adventi.

During Peter's time at Archangels, its processes and rules of engagement were largely set and still remain. The flair and intuition that hallmarked Barry and Mike's style have been embedded in the syndicate, and so it should remain. Archangels was now widely recognised as the pre-eminent investor in early-stage companies in Scotland.

Barry Sealey (left) and Mike Rutterford in 1997... (© *Studio 16*)

...and in 2017.

Above: Mike at the office in Edinburgh.

Below: Barry, 2017 portrait.

Opposite, below: launch of the Strathclyde University report, September 2015, L–R: Eric Young (chairman), Mike Rutterford, David Ovens, John Waddell.

Above: John Waddell,
CEO 2005–2015.

Right: the leadership team 2017,
L–R: Sarah Hardy, David Ovens,
Niki McKenzie.

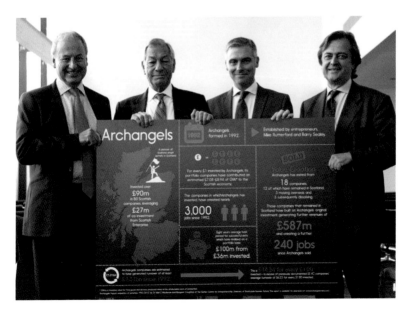

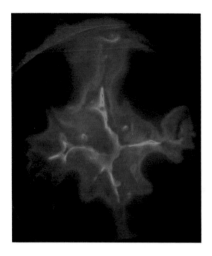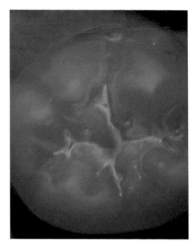

Above: images generated by Calcivis imaging system depicting active tooth demineralisation. (© *Calcivis*)

Below: a technician with Calcivis equipment. (© *Calcivis*)

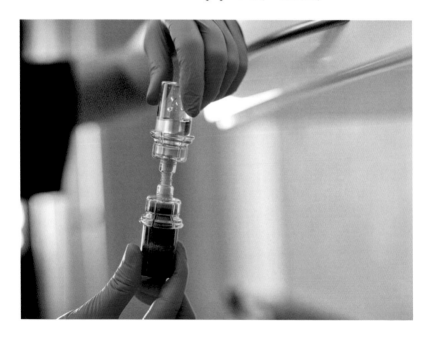

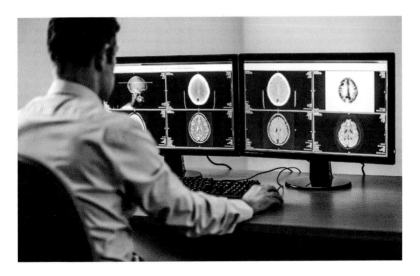

Above: Blackford imaging system. (© *Blackford Analysis*)

Below: Leif Anderson, whose retinal detachment inspired his father, Douglas Anderson, to create the Optomap machine, commercialised by Optos.

Above: Scotland's Deputy First Minister, John Swinney (left), and Archangels' Mike Rutterford pictured with Touch bionic hands; and *below*: skydiver Claudia wearing her bionic hand. (© *Touch Bionics*)

Above: an Arrayjet bio-printing instrument. (© *Arrayjet*)

Below: Critiqom: production floor. (© *Critiqom*)

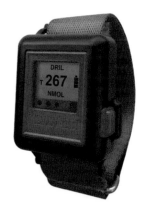

iSTAR 360° Panoramic
Camera. (© *NCTech*)

HAVWEAR. (© *Reactec*)

PowerPhotonic. (© *PowerPhotonic*)

5

THE OPTOS STORY

"The Panoramic 200 is now recognised as the only instrument that allows for the detection and differential diagnosis of most retinal abnormalities, in most patients, in just minutes without either pupillary dilation or patient discomfort. The Panoramic 200 is superb at initially finding a lesion."

Panoramic Ophthalmoscopy,

2007

The story of Optos is inextricably woven into the fabric of Archangels. From the first meeting between Douglas Anderson, the inventor, and Barry Sealey in July 1992, until the full stock market flotation of the company in February 2006, Optos would absorb a huge amount of time and money for Archangels. But the result was eventually highly successful both in terms of the ground-breaking science the company achieved and the financial reward for founders and shareholders.

Douglas Anderson is an industrial designer, but he is

also an indefatigable adventurer who set up his design company, Crombie Anderson, in 1982 as a way to subsidise his passions for exploring, mountain climbing, sailing and wilderness pursuits. He is undoubtedly a very clever industrial designer and his consultancy business gave birth to a number of products, some of which he spun out of his own company.

But the genesis of the idea that would become Optos was to arise from a very personal experience. Douglas's son, Leif, had lost his sight in one eye at the age of five, having suffered a retinal detachment that was not detected in time, despite undergoing regular eye examinations. These examinations were uncomfortable procedures for a child, involving drops in the eye, and making it almost impossible for a doctor to conduct a complete examination and view the entire retina. Douglas was angry and frustrated by the lack of a more efficient method of eye examination and vowed to find a solution.

And so Douglas began work on designing a prototype of a machine that would allow the full retina to be examined without the need for eye drops. His original plan was to avoid the use of venture capitalists, with which he had become somewhat disenchanted, and purely sell on his prototype for manufacture and commercialisation by a third party. However, even this needed to be financed somehow and he was introduced to Barry by Sandy Finlayson.

The first meeting between Douglas and Barry was somewhat stormy, as might be expected from two such strong characters. Douglas told Barry that the problem he was trying to solve arose from "the ridiculously primitive backwater of medical imaging" and that his very early stabs at finding a solution would work. Barry was hugely sceptical.

"Why on earth do you think that you can do anything about this when there are thousands of other eminently qualified people in this field? As far as I understand from what you have told me, you know nothing about optics or ophthalmology."

To which Douglas responded, "Correct, I am not an optical expert. But I've got a lot of experience of developing medical products in general and I'd like to have a go, so why don't you give me some money?" Not an auspicious start, but Barry was intrigued enough to find out more.

Barry's brother-in-law, Michael Walsh, was an ophthalmic surgeon in Perth in Western Australia, so that evening Barry called him. "It sounds quite amazing. I suggest you go ahead and write the cheque," was his advice. And so Barry undertook to try to raise the necessary money.

There was no business plan at that stage, so Barry prepared his own note of the stages of development that would be required, including the market research, preparation of a proper business plan, development of a prototype, pre-production development, satisfaction of regulatory requirements and so on. He recognised that the initial seed investment required of around £80,000 would need to be followed, probably from investing institutions, by further investment of £1–2 million. He circulated his note round a few colleagues and invited them to a presentation and discussion on the project at the offices of Crombie Anderson in Fife. Mike, of course, was involved and he, Barry and a few others journeyed to Fife in August 1992 to see the presentation.

The result of the presentation was unanimous acclaim and a desire to proceed to support the initial requirements. In fact, at the presentation, Barry had volunteered to pretend to be a patient and Douglas had pretended to be the doctor using a pencil instead of an ophthalmoscope to show the complete ineffectiveness of the procedure. He likened his solution to a doctor looking for a nail in a dark room using a pencil torch compared to his solution, which would be like switching on the light to see the whole room all at once. This story was to become part of the folklore of Optos.

Thereafter, Barry wrote to those who had attended the presentation and within a month the required £80,000 had been raised and the company was funded, with the investors holding 51% of the equity and Crombie Anderson holding the remaining 49%. The £80,000 also released a SMART (Small Firms' Merit Award for Research and Technology) award of £40,000, giving the company a pot of £120,000 to start work.

And so the starting gun was fired. But this was to be no 100-metre dash; rather, it was to be a gruelling marathon beyond the imaginings of the initial investors. A company was formed, called BESCA; Barry became chairman and

Mike joined the board along with Douglas. A project team was set up within Crombie Anderson to begin the task of designing the first prototype.

But the first project team failed to come up with a viable solution and so a second team was formed, which also failed. However, the investors did not lose faith and were prepared to inject further cash to enable a third team to be put together within the company and this time a potential product solution emerged.

At this stage, in 1995, it was clear that the product, in prototype form, was becoming commercially viable but that it was very unlikely that enough funding would be available to manufacture and distribute the product within the company and therefore the company should be sold to allow someone else to take it forward. Significant interest was shown by a Swiss optical company, but the deal fell through and the management team and investors now faced a huge decision as to whether they could indeed commercialise the product themselves.

In April 1996, confidence was growing and the company was renamed Optos; the following February it was re-registered as a public limited company, becoming Optos plc, with an emerging view that a flotation on AIM, the junior market, might be a possible exit opportunity.

Part of this optimism arose from the appointment to the board of Patrick Paul, a successful entrepreneur in the medical device industry who had built and sold companies in the USA and saw an opportunity in Optos. Patrick was initially brought onto the board to advise on possible exit strategies, but his first solution to the funding problem was critical and effective. Basically, he suggested a 'pay-per-customer' model, which was attached to a three-year leasing agreement that could be funded upfront by financial institutions. This leasing/funding model was called Access Technology Now and two institutions, Citigroup and Rabobank, agreed to provide the funding to build the machines.

"This model was the basis of the success of the company," said former CEO Stephane Sallmard. "We shared revenue with the doctors, which was extremely positive, and we had revenues guaranteed for the second and third years which could be financed through the banks."

Patrick also put his money where his mouth was and became a significant investor in 1997, when it was recognised that, although a financially sustainable model was in place to fund the manufacture and sales of machines, a new infrastructure for the company was required to build critical mass globally.

At the same time as Patrick's appointment, another hugely influential appointment was made. Anne Glover had spent many years at the sharp end of investment in early stage companies, both in the USA and the UK. She had become a business angel in her own right but had her eye on setting up a venture capital fund to invest in small-cap technology companies. At the time she became aware of Optos, she was working from a desk in the offices of Montanaro in London near to Peter Searight, the manager of the newly created UK Smaller Companies

Investment Trust plc. Peter had received the papers on Optos from Bell Lawrie, the Glasgow stockbrokers, and passed them on to Anne for review. It was agreed that it was a sufficiently interesting proposal to justify Anne doing due diligence on the company and reporting back to Peter for a final decision. It was decided that an investment was appropriate on the condition that Anne joined the board and that there was a real chance of flotation within a couple of years.

Montanaro invested £1 million along with Rothschilds, and Anne personally invested £25,000 and joined the board. Remarkably, the Montanaro investment contained no special terms and they invested shoulder to shoulder with the existing angel investors, which pleased Barry and the others enormously. Anne even passed the test of being 'interviewed' by Douglas Anderson as to her suitability to be a director, which Anne found hilarious in the circumstances.

Over the next two years, Anne consummated her dream of setting up a technology fund by creating Amadeus Capital Partners, which was to become a staunch and unremitting supporter of Optos throughout all the years leading to eventual flotation and which would again invest on the same terms as the angel investors.

The final new appointment to the board was to be Ann Gloag, who, along with her brother Brian Souter, had been a very supportive investor in Optos from the early days.

And so a powerful board was formed to guide the company through to an eventual exit, and an unusual partnership was formed between business angels and venture capitalists that was to prove invaluable in the years ahead.

For the next few years, the company fine-tuned the development of its first machine, the Panoramic 200, beginning clinical trials in 1998 and achieving FDA approval in the USA in February 1999.

The Panoramic 200 generated an optomap retinal image, which enabled the practitioner to view a substantial portion of the retina at once with a single camera snapshot that took a quarter of a second and was entirely non-invasive with no eye drops needed. It meant the prospect of early detection of non-eye diseases such as diabetes, glaucoma, hypertension and certain cancers. It was truly revolutionary.

The company was also fine-tuning its business model with the help of Patrick Paul. The key to the sale of machines was not just in the leasing arrangements but, critically, in the 'pay per customer' approach, where Patrick hammered home the message that the most important sales point was the push towards selling optomaps as an application software company rather than as a capital equipment company.

The first machine was leased in August 1999 to Lou Frank, an optometrist near Boston as it was recognised that the USA would be the key marketplace for the development of the company.

But the necessary development and growth of the

company was beginning to use serious amounts of cash and, in October 2000, the board appointed ING Barings to assist in raising funds of up to £20 million and preparing documentation to move towards a pre-IPO placing, to be followed by a listing on AIM. There was significant interest from three large institutions, but the global economic picture was deteriorating quickly and, by mid-2001, it was becoming clear that pre-IPO fundraising was unlikely.

During this time there was an enormous strain on cashflow and the investors were required to put in significant sums of money on an almost monthly basis to ensure that wages were paid and that the company could continue trading. Indeed, in the period from January 2000 to August 2001, Barry alone injected a significant sum to keep the company going and he was supported in this by Mike, Patrick, Brian Souter and Ann Gloag.

In 1998 the executive team had been strengthened by the appointment of Ian Stevens as finance director and Steve Guida, who was hired to set up the American operations. Ian was to prove invaluable to the company as he juggled the finances and was subsequently asked to run the US operations in 2002.

In 2001 it was agreed that the complexities of the company demanded an experienced chief executive and, after a head-hunting search, Stephane Sallmard was appointed as CEO in June 2001. Stephane, a Frenchman who holds a masters in electronic engineering and completed a management programme at the Kellogg School of management at Northwestern University, has had an impressive career, having worked for 30 years in the medical and technology arena with companies such as Acuson, GE Medical, Siemens Nixdorf, Digital and IBM. He had most recently been managing director of the Paris-based technology company Lectra Systems. Stephane brought huge and much-needed experience to Optos at a critical time. Given the importance of his appointment and the difficult cash position in the company, Patrick agreed to underwrite the first 12 months of Stephane's contract.

Interestingly, this can sometimes be a difficult time of change in a growing company. Often the founder will resist the idea of an 'outsider' coming in to run 'his' company but it is an important step to take if the company is to flourish and the required skills put in place for the future. In this case, Douglas Anderson was fully supportive of Stephane's appointment and the two worked well together.

Given the failure of the plan to raise money and list on AIM, it was clear that the position was desperate. On 4 July 2001, Barry wrote to shareholders and other interested parties in an attempt to raise sufficient funds to keep the company going. Stephane's arrival in June had begun with a cost-reduction plan and Barry wrote in his letter, *"All of the steps which Stephane has taken will reduce the risks associated with the business. Nonetheless, we are still in urgent need of funds. In the very short term our objective is to raise a minimum of £2.5 million which should cover operating costs through to the early part of 2002."* Barry said that a further £2.5 million would help see them through until September 2002 and invited everyone to a meeting at the Optos office in Dunfermline on Thursday, 19 July.

Some 50 people turned up to that meeting, including investors, other wealthy individuals and some institutional investors who had flown up from London with Anne Glover. Barry began the meeting by introducing Stephane as the new chief executive who, in turn, assured the meeting that he was committed to staying on as CEO despite the difficulties, which was a crucial statement to make.

Barry then spelled out the reality of the situation. The good news was that the market for ophthalmoscope machines, particularly in the USA and Germany, was increasing and, while there were some competitor machines available, third-party endorsement was now recognising that the Optos machine was superior in many ways to its rivals. The company was expected to break even before the end of 2002 and, despite the recent failure to secure a listing on AIM, there remained a glimmer of hope of an IPO in the medium term. The company needed £5 million to create some breathing space and cover working capital requirements as well as essential overheads.

The meeting received this report calmly and was generally very supportive of carrying on. But there was a robust discussion of the price at which any such investment would take place. The previous round of funding had taken place at 72.5p per share but there were strong opinions expressed that this should be a significant 'down' round and eventually a price of 40p began to emerge. There was a danger that the meeting was getting bogged down in a discussion of price and the capital intensiveness of the business model until an extraordinary intervention by June Rutterford, who had been sitting quietly beside Mike, brought things sharply back into focus.

June was normally quiet at this kind of meeting but, on this occasion, she took a deep breath, stood up and said, "Look, we've really had enough discussion. If we leave here today and nothing is resolved, the company will struggle to survive. If everyone writes down on a piece of paper how much they are prepared to invest and put it in a hat, then we can get somewhere." She further declared, "Count me in. I'm going to invest."

There was a collective gasp from the room and some of the London-based investors just couldn't believe what they were seeing. But it worked and the successful seal was put on it by Gavin Gemmell, who had not previously invested in Optos, but who rose from his seat and declared that he would invest £400,000.

Over the next ten minutes, pieces of paper were passed round and then dropped into a hat, much like a hushed Church of Scotland Sunday collection. Barry and Stephane disappeared behind a screen and re-emerged some minutes later to say that pledges had been received for £1.5 million and that they therefore had the confidence to progress with a formal rights issue.

This really was an extraordinary and entirely unexpected outcome. June Rutterford recalled, "I knew the way the meeting was going and we were all going to leave the room and nothing would get sorted. As soon as you leave a meeting room, it stops being a priority and other matters fill the gap. We needed to resolve the issue there and then for the sake of the company."

Barry wrote to all of the shareholders telling them of the outcome of the meeting: *"Your board has determined to do a share placing at the significantly discounted price of 40p per share. We have determined that this placing should only go ahead if we can secure a minimum of £2 million which will give us adequate time to make other arrangements. Our hope, however, would be to raise more to give us greater security as we move forward."* In fact, that round raised £3 million and was further augmented in November of that year with agreement of a loan from the Bank of Scotland of £5 million.

Of course that wasn't the end of the fundraising requirements, but it was a crucial turning point. Amadeus, which had not been able to invest in the July 2001 round for technical reasons, was to put in a further £10 million in the years ahead, showing incredible support for this strongly emerging company.

In 2004 it was becoming apparent that Optos was nearing the stage where it could be floated. An earlier stipulation by Anne Glover meant that such a flotation should be on the main FTSE market and not AIM, the junior market. This would require big guns to achieve it and Anne had spent some time warming up the big boys for the event.

In October 2004 the Optos board carried out a beauty parade of the key banks that might lead the flotation and plumped for Goldman Sachs as the best contender. Its analyst, Hans Boström, was clearly a fan of the company and, within weeks, Goldman Sachs produced a plan for the flotation and a valuation range that impressed the board.

Barry, as always, was mindful of the huge fees that investment banks earned from these transactions, but it was clear that Goldman Sachs would earn its corn from the work it put into the pre-flotation stage and, indeed, the price at which the company would eventually be floated. The market conditions were relatively favourable for small-cap companies and the timing was good.

As is almost inevitable in the lead-up to a major IPO, the board had to undergo changes. In November 1995, John Padfield joined the board as a non-executive director and chairman designate. On 31 December 2005, Barry stepped down and John took over as chairman. In the same month, Mike and Ann Gloag stepped down from the board and on 1 January 2006, Barry Rose joined as a non-executive director. These were necessary changes ahead of flotation but, nevertheless, they were quite difficult for those involved, who had seen the company through all the ups and downs of the previous 14 years, to undertake.

Finally, on 15 February 2006, Optos was listed on the FTSE market, having raised £30 million in the process and emerging with a market value of £165 million. At that stage, Optos had a turnover of £41 million, employed 230 people and became one of the few Scottish companies quoted on the FTSE main market.

All of the investors finally made money, although there were restrictions on how many shares they could sell at flotation and the variability of the share price thereafter makes it difficult to be precise about how much each investor really made. Barry had invested around £750,000 over the years and was able to cover that on flotation by selling just 15% of his holding. This suggests a return of 667% on his investment at the time of flotation.

For all the difficult times and hard decisions, Optos and the people involved justified their tenacity and commit-ment. It was, perhaps, not a normal example of business angel investment and is unlikely to be repeated in modern times, but it did show how VCs and angels can work together to create a business of real value from which many people, not least the patients, continue to benefit.

In March 2015, Optos was awarded the 2014 Technology of the Year Award at the UK PLC Awards in London. The presentation followed in the wake of an announce-ment by the boards of directors of Nikon and Optos on 27 February 2015 that they had agreed the terms of a recom-mended cash offer to be made by Nikon for the entire share capital of Optos. Under the terms of the transaction, Optos shareholders were entitled to receive 340 pence in cash for each Optos share. The transaction valued the entire share capital of Optos at £259.3 million.

In December 2016 Nikon and Optos announced an agreement for an exclusive collaboration with Verily, formerly known as Google Life Sciences, to combine its leadership in optical engineering, proprietary ultra-widefield technology and strong commercial presence among eyecare specialists, and Verily's machine learning-enabled technology. The goal of this collaboration is to create technology and solutions to further enhance retinal screening for diabetic retinopathy and diabetic macular oedema. This innovation is intended to assist in the efficient referral of patients to eyecare specialists and in providing these specialists with assisted reading programs for the easier diagnosis of disease.

6

COMING OF AGE

John Waddell became chief executive of Archangels in 2005. His background was very different from both Juliette Chapman and Peter Shakeshaft and allowed him to bring to bear a more professional approach to syndicate decisions that had been a necessary step for what was now a substantial business.

Born in Inverness, John graduated as a lawyer from Edinburgh University in 1978 and served his indenture with Simpson Kinnimont & Maxwell. He moved in 1980 to Steedman Ramage, where he became a partner in 1983 and began his specialisation in corporate work, particularly deal-making. But John was keen to get out of the purely professional life and, in January 1986, joined Christian Salvesen and was immediately put to work by Barry Sealey on a series of complex business deals, which suited John down to the ground.

Salvesen had become a publicly quoted company the previous year and John worked around the world, buying and selling companies for Salvesen, enjoying a high level of autonomy, which was a tremendous experience. His final deal was the demerger of Aggreko in September 1997, by which point he had carried out an astonishing 66 deals for the company.

John left Salvesen immediately after the demerger of Aggreko and, after a brief period in Provence with his family, re-entered the fray by joining the international division of Bank of Scotland, where he resumed his overseas travelling. In 2000 he joined Noble Grossart, the highly respected Scottish merchant bank, where he worked with Sir Angus Grossart and Sir Ewan Brown.

However, by the autumn of 2004, John was ready for something else and he approached his old Salvesen boss, Barry Sealey, seeking guidance and ideas. Barry was aware that Peter Shakeshaft was thinking of stepping back, though there was no rush, which also suited John since he needed some time to consider whether Archangels would be the right move for him. In the end it all worked out very well, with Peter able to step away from executive management completely, which is what he really wanted to do, and John taking over as chief executive.

John started in June 2005. Once he settled into his new position and Archangels' companies were assured about his intentions, he would steer a more radical Archangels investment approach, tapping into international connections and seeking closer ties with an array of venture capital organisations.

Under John's stewardship, Archangels refined its investment approach to focus on early-stage companies in the technology and life sciences sectors, with investee companies required to have high growth and international sales potential with defensible technology and clear intellectual property. Further, they had to be based in Scotland and in a sector that qualified under the Enterprise Investment Scheme (EIS). Archangels' clear preference was to invest in companies that were not capital intensive and were capable of achieving scale and generating revenues without significant capital expenditure.

John's tenure as chief executive has seen a period of significant activity for the syndicate. On average, each year Archangels now receives between 100 and 150 business plans. From these enquiries, it will typically invest in only two or three new deals each year, with the remainder of its funding being committed to existing portfolio companies. New deals usually represent around 10–20% of funds invested each year.

This increased activity necessitated more resources and John quickly set about putting in place a professional investment team to act as gatekeeper for Archangels and undertake the initial screening of all potential investments. This involves filtering businesses against Archangels' key investment criteria, assessing the business plan and, most importantly, meeting the entrepreneur to gather information about the team and the company. However, where there is specific domain expertise within the Archangels' syndicate, or its wider network, the investment team may call on that experience and knowledge at this stage.

The businesses that get through the filtering and initial screening processes are then evaluated in detail by Archangels' investment committee, its board of directors. This process includes a presentation by the company to the investment committee, which will make a collective decision on whether or not to invest in the business. If the board decides unanimously to invest, then the opportunity is opened up to the rest of the group for each member to decide individually whether they also wish to invest. However, the board will itself invest at least £100,000 in any new deal.

Prior to proposing any funding for a company, whether initial or follow on, Archangels members will know that the funding proposition has been scrutinised by its investment team and has the support of its board. Companies prepare an investor presentation and all Archangels members are invited to attend with a view to making a personal investment decision.

Following the investor presentation, Archangels' investment team liaises with the members and the company to deal with any queries raised by the syndicate, with a view to building the investment book. All funds invested by Archangels into portfolio companies come directly from its members, who can choose to invest in any or none of the portfolio companies. In essence, members create their own portfolios.

At the point of investment, Archangels always seeks to understand the potential overall investment requirement through to value inflection and makes sure its members plan for these important follow-on rounds. As a result, it has a strong track record of supporting its companies through all their funding rounds.

Archangels takes a rigorous approach to the management of its portfolio companies, maintaining a regular, active dialogue with each. It takes observer rights in all companies, and investment executives attend board meetings. It also requires its companies to produce monthly management accounts and to report on a quarterly basis to Archangels and all shareholders, incorporating commentary on the financial position of the company, commercial issues and strategic developments as well as operational issues.

The most important output from Archangels' pre-investment due diligence process is to develop a strong relationship with the management team. This relationship develops further after the investment is made. Archangels ensures that a strong non-executive board is in place to provide good governance as well as conduct an effective interrogation of and challenge to management's strategy.

At a company-specific level, Archangels encourages and supports its management teams, but it is prepared to intervene where this is required to add value or to prevent the destruction of shareholder value. This may involve putting in place more appropriate executive or non-executive resources, providing additional support to the incumbent management team, providing access to technical expertise that will allow the company to access export or other markets, or anything else which leverages the knowledge and experience of the Archangels network. It also encourages management teams to plan their exit strategy from an early stage and develop contacts with potential purchasers so that there is an awareness of what Archangels' companies do.

When John Waddell analysed a prospective investee company, in conjunction with the board and the executives, the question he would seek to answer was: 'How much is the company going to be worth in three years' time?'

A huge amount of work is done in assessing the business plan and calculating the value, with particular focus on the possible market and potential sales. Gavin Gemmell is firm about the board and the management both willingly signing up to the pricing.

"You sometimes get people saying they are giving away too much of their business at too low a price. I usually say, 'Look, as an executive of the company you can make money in several ways: you can get a salary, you might get a performance bonus, or some share options, but we as investors can only make money on our ordinary shares."

He will also remind those who are falling behind on their business plan that a venture capitalist would almost certainly wipe out their stake as they put in more money.

"It is almost inevitable that a company will come back for further rounds of funding," explained John's investment colleague, Mary Jane Brouwers. "It does depend on what is happening in the business. They might have an amazing sales opportunity with customers, but if the firm wants to deliver, they need to invest to secure that opportunity."

There is a standard investment agreement that lays out Archangels' requirements. These are often prepared by Stuart Hendry or one of his colleagues at MBM Commercial. Stuart Hendry's involvement with Archangels stretches back to the Internet Flower Company, Peter Shakeshaft's first deal.

"Archangels has retained standard legal documents, so it tries to keep the variations to a minimum," she said. "A large number of deals go through on standard terms, but there are a few that get more complex with multiple investing partners."

Sandy Finlayson's original 15-page investment agreement, which was pared down from around 80, has since crept up to 45 pages.

John and the team at Archangels also brought rigour to the exit process, which, aside from dividends, was the only source of value creation for members. If a company is being sold, each investor makes his or her own decision about whether to sell his or her shares, although the investment agreement will allow the majority to 'drag along' the reluctant minority, if need be.

To facilitate and expedite the exit process, Archangels' members grant a power of attorney in favour of the investment team. It was Gavin Gemmell who suggested and instigated this process and the fact that Archangels has had a number of high-profile exits in recent years has meant that the syndicate has remained highly engaged.

There are a number of Archangels meetings each year. The most notable event, Chorus, meets once a year and serves multiple purposes. It provides training sessions for the management teams, as well as a showcase of all the portfolio companies followed by a dinner where investors, company executives, invited guests and potential new syndicate members can mingle.

"We thought it was important to bring all our investors together and meet the companies," said Barry Sealey. "The first time was in the 19th-century Merchants Hall in Hanover Street, Edinburgh. We invited all our companies and investors and held a very pleasant reception then a sit-down dinner. It worked so well that we've done it ever since."

Mike added, "The physical introduction of companies means they have common customers and shared interests. I think that our companies are 'cousins' in the same family of Archangels," he said.

Chorus speakers have included Wendy Alexander, the former Scottish Enterprise and Lifelong Minister; Jim McColl, the serial entrepreneur; and Sir John Elvidge, the top Scottish civil servant and now chair of Edinburgh Airport. One famous person who failed to turn up was Scotland's then First Minister, Alex Salmond, although a civil servant delivered his pre-prepared speech.

The Chorus event is now held at the Dovecot Studios, a stone's throw from Edinburgh University's Old College. Alastair Salvesen and his wife have been big supporters and directors of the Dovecot Studios, helping to transform a municipal swimming baths in Edinburgh into a modern art space and workshops.

Barry's own swansong was in March 2011 at an Archangels Chorus where he thanked the entrepreneurs who have generated so many innovations and kept the spirit of enterprise alive in Scotland and referred to Archangels as "a great partnership between innovators and investors".

7

OPEN-DOOR POLICY FOR YOLLIES

Having strengthened the Archangels' investment process, John Waddell now wanted to establish proper peer benchmarking of the performance of Archangels' portfolio. He approached the University of Edinburgh Business School and spoke to Dr Geoff Gregson, a lecturer in entrepreneurship and innovation, about setting up a robust independent study.

Dr Gregson identified two academic partnership programmes that could provide resources for Archangels to allow this benchmarking to be done: the Knowledge Transfer Partnerships and the Ewing Marion Kauffman Foundation, the latter founded by pharmaceutical businessman Ewing Kauffman, which runs leadership programmes to support emerging entrepreneurs.

The Knowledge Transfer Partnerships was a UK-wide programme designed to bring academics closer to industry, while the Kauffman Fellows Program was more specific in helping to teach technical and scientific personnel about the venture capital and finance industry. With funding agreed and supported by Edinburgh University, a position with Archangels was advertised in February 2007 and Sacha Mann, a Canadian chemistry graduate with an MBA and a masters in biotechnology, was the successful applicant. She had already taken her first steps in the venture capital industry in Vancouver, working with technology transfer in start-ups.

Sacha arrived in Edinburgh in August 2007. She spent two years on her programmes working with Archangels, which she recalls as being an immensely rewarding 'hands-on' experience in a very busy office.

"My research showed that Archangels was definitely punching well above its weight," she said. "I attended several conferences and met angel syndicates from Holland, Scandinavia, Australia, New Zealand, in the rest of the UK, and groups on the east and west coasts of America. We compared notes about our success rates. What we found was that Archangels was considered highly successful, with a rich history and a very supportive inner circle, and was said to be one of the best syndicates in Europe, if not the world."

The success of Archangels was also starting to be realised at home. In that same year, 2007, the work of Barry and Mike was formally recognised by the Entrepreneurial Exchange at its annual awards ceremony at the Hilton Hotel in Glasgow. Both men stepped up onto the stage to collect their awards. Barry spoke first and delivered an eloquent speech of appreciation, praising the organisers, and saying a few well-chosen words about the progress of several of Archangels' investments. He then stepped aside and Mike delivered the shortest speech in the award's history.

"We deserve it!" he said. The audience of 700 burst into laughter at such a brazen acceptance.

With Optos now established as a fully-fledged international company, and a growing recognition of the importance of the syndicate, Archangels developed self-confidence and a strong reputation, coupled with a professionalism and an ability to help companies. It continued its open-door policy, willing to see potential entrepreneurs looking for equity funding in the high-growth technology and life science sectors in Scotland.

The word 'Yollies' had been coined to refer to 'young leading innovative companies', and a phone-call to John Waddell was often enough to secure at least an initial meeting. One 'Yollie' that came to Archangels through this route was Vitrology, formed as a biopharmaceutical contract testing organisation in April 2007. The founders had worked for BioReliance, then owned by Avista Capital Partners, a private equity company, and were unhappy with the way it was run and its poor service levels. They decided that, if they could raise the money, they could easily do it better themselves. So they approached Archangels, which rallied round to raise funding for this West of Scotland biotechnology start-up.

The management team already knew its customers, which gave the business a head start. They had also identified a vacant biomedical research facility in Clydebank, outside Glasgow, which had been fitted out, but required specialist development for cell and virus culture and in-vitro agent testing. By January 2008, the company had completed the refurbishment of Clydebank Business Park, which was inspected and then accepted into the Good Laboratory Practice programmes (GLP) of the UK Medical and Healthcare product agency. The high-tech laboratories allowed Vitrology to begin a contract testing service for the big pharma companies. This accreditation was vital to satisfy major regulatory authorities, including the powerful US Food and Drug Administration (FDA) and its European equivalent, the European Medicines Agency.

"The day I saw Vitrology's business plan I said it was the best one I had seen. I told Archangels' board, 'I think we should back it! And I will tell you who will buy it: SGS,'" recalled Ian Sword.

"I liked the team. They were in the same space as I had been and they were focused on a niche, but I had to resolve a delicate issue with the chairman, who was a former colleague."

Vitrology's then chairman had worked with Ian Sword at Inveresk and Amersham International. He had been a senior director and had enjoyed a successful career inside a major corporate, but the company needed a different kind of leadership and it fell to Ian Sword to ask him to go. Ian brought in a new chair, Dr Harry Draffan, and a new board of directors that proved to be very effective. Indeed, in November 2008, with 20 experienced scientific staff, Vitrology was named as Scotland's 'most promising young life science company'.

As the company grew, it required a further £500,000 from Archangels. In its third year, Vitrology broke even, a massive achievement for a biotechnology firm, and by its fourth year, having landed a major project, delivered decent profits.

Just as Ian Sword had predicted, Vitrology was indeed sold to SGS, a Swiss company listed in Geneva with a substantial UK presence, in May 2012.

In February 2010 another of the 'Yollies', MGB Biopharma, a spin-out from the University of Strathclyde in Glasgow, was able to secure more than £2.2 million from Archangels, in association with the Scottish Co-investment Fund, TRI Cap and Barwell for pre-clinical work in fighting diseases with a new type of antibacterial compound. The start-up capital was for the biopharmaceutical drug discovery company set up in 2009 to develop a new breed of medicines. Sacha Mann undertook the due diligence and helped with the fundraising.

"It was taking a long time to raise the funding," she said. "When the financial industry was crumbling, there were ramifications for all kinds of companies looking for funding."

Sacha regarded this as an opportunity and proposed that, with a relatively small investment of £2 million, the scientists could capture some useful data that could create some value. The company name MGB comes from compounds known as DNA minor groove binders. One of its challenges was to develop an antibiotic compound that effectively treats the resistant strains of *Clostridium difficile* (*C. Diff*), a cause of infection in hospitals and among elderly people. The technology was licensed from the University of Strathclyde, with help from the Synergy Fund, a collaboration of Strathclyde and Glasgow universities, and Scottish Enterprise's Proof of Concept fund. According to John Waddell, this was one of the largest deals that Archangels had ever led and one of the most complex.

MGB's management team includes chief executive Miroslav Ravic, from Belgrade, who has a PhD in clinical pharmacology and is the author of several scientific papers. Miroslav had been working in clinical research and had teamed up with Gavin Clark, a Scottish chemist who worked with GlaxoWellcome and Tibotec pharmaceuticals, bought by Johnson & Johnson in 2002. He had been a consultant in a number of rounds of fundraising and in the licensing of key technology. The chairman, Adam Christie, had a long career in pharma companies, having worked on the sale of PowderMed to Pfizer in 2006.

In September 2015, MGB Biopharma's role in developing a truly novel class of anti-infectives to address the major global problem of antibiotic resistance was recognised when it was named a Winner in the 2015 Scottish Business Insider Deals & Dealmakers Awards. Judging criteria included the quality of the investment capital, the level and complexity of the syndication of the investment, the scale of market opportunity for the company and potential return for investors, and the role of the management team and its advisers in realising the deal.

Accepting the award, Miroslav, CEO of MGB Biopharma, said, "We believe that our novel candidate, which originated from the University of Strathclyde, has the potential to transform antimicrobial resistance, by bringing true novelty to the market, not seen for over a decade."

Vitrology and MGB Biopharma are just two of the many 'Yollies' to have benefited from Archangels open-door policy.

8

IT'S NICE TO BE AN ANGEL

Barry Sealey is an opportunist. He often repeats his view that business is about "seeing and seizing an opportunity" and his business life proves this. He has seldom missed a chance to put people together in a genuine desire to help aspiring entrepreneurs. While he is not a party political person, he has consistently sought to ensure that Archangels' activities in helping start-up companies are properly understood by senior politicians. On this score, Mike Rutterford is in agreement with Barry that policymakers of whatever hue must understand and appreciate the difficulties of building successful businesses.

So getting the Chancellor of the Exchequer along for an early-morning coffee was no mean feat. Mike had been sailing his boat around the West Coast of Scotland and landed at Plockton with clatter and fanfare. On the quayside he had bumped into Catherine MacLeod, an old school friend of John Waddell's brother from Inverness Royal Academy. She turned out to be a former political journalist from the Westminster lobby and special adviser to the Chancellor. When Mike got back to Edinburgh he organised a mini-reunion with John.

Some weeks later, during the Edinburgh Festival in August 2007, Barry was invited to a drinks reception at Scotland House on Melville Street, the office of the Secretary of State for Scotland in the Westminster government. It was a gathering of business suits hosted by the Scottish Secretary and a chance to meet the new Chancellor of the Exchequer, Alistair Darling, who had been appointed by the new Prime Minister Gordon Brown in June.

Catherine MacLeod introduced Alistair Darling to Barry, who wasted no time in inviting the Chancellor to come and see Archangels' set-up. Within weeks, there were other pressing tasks for the Chancellor as Northern Rock bank collapsed, yet he kept his word.

Sacha Mann recalled a good-natured encounter between Barry, John and Alistair Darling on 14 January 2008, when the Chancellor dropped in for a breakfast coffee and bacon rolls to hear what Archangels was doing to support UK business. Typically, Barry did not miss an opportunity to follow up, writing to the Treasury on 31 January 2008, raising the key points of the meeting and noting that EIS, CVS and Reinvestment Relief schemes had been extremely important to the support of early-stage companies.

"As with all taxation arrangements, they take a while to become fully appreciated and used and, not least for this reason, we are always concerned with changes."

Barry wrote that the introduction of the European Commission rules to restrict EIS relief to companies with fewer than 50 employees and to investment of less than £2 million was unduly restrictive, given the increasing cost of getting from start-up to market, and stated that Archangels was concerned at HMRC's vigorous attempts to restrict the use of EIS.

> *"One of our companies, Optos plc, which was a great success story for Scotland, was founded in 1992 and still does not have its EIS position fully resolved despite an appeal to . . . the General Commissioners."*

Barry praised the Scottish Co-investment Fund, saying it was a useful model for other parts of the United Kingdom, but he suggested that it too would benefit from stability rather than change. He also wrote about the difficulties of young companies securing public procurement contracts, mirroring Mike's regular plea to: 'Give us an order, not a grant'.

> *"Despite some efforts to improve the situation, we feel we are still a long way from giving the support that could be both practical for the company and, in many cases, beneficial to the user organisation and the Exchequer."*

In a highly topical point, Barry wrote that Archangels was concerned at the reluctance of banks to support young companies, even with the availability of the Small Firms

Loan Guarantee Scheme, observing that this was a real failure of a well-intentioned and potentially valuable scheme. He also expressed frustration at the commercialisation departments of some of Scotland's leading universities.

"There has also been a trend towards universities making exclusive agreements with venture capital groups which, in our view, are distinctly anti-competitive and in the longer term damaging both to the university and to the generation of new enterprise."

Barry wrote that he felt it inappropriate to raise the subject of Capital Gains Tax at their meeting but said the recent relief for entrepreneurs was welcome.

"However, we are still disappointed with the original change on two counts. First, the removal of the distinction between long and short term investment seems to be a nod in favour of the speculators rather than the true investors. Secondly, the removal of the common rate of 40% in capital gains tax and income tax may encourage the return of schemes to convert income into capital."

What Archangels wanted was to ensure that the tax relief did what it was intended to do: encourage young companies and not some spurious tax-evading sleight of hand. These were all important issues affecting the work of Archangels and particularly pertinent was Barry's point that major banks were not lending to small businesses. However, Alistair Darling might be forgiven for handing Barry's letter over to a suitable Treasury official rather than dealing with it himself as he was just about to face dealing with the collapse of Northern Rock bank – which would be taken into public ownership a few days later – and the full-blown banking crisis that was set to engulf the United States and Britain.

A few years later there was mounting evidence to suggest that politicians had begun to appreciate the importance of angel syndicates as drivers for the economy. In September 2010, some key civil servants invited John Waddell, Sandy Finlayson and Ian Ritchie to a brainstorming session at the Department of Business, Innovation and Skills (BIS) in London sparked by Colin Mason's academic study about the success of the business angel networks in Scotland.

Around 40 people gathered, with Lord Young of Graffham, a special business adviser to David Cameron at the time, among the group. By way of introduction, a BIS official said that government can do one of three things: tax, spend or regulate. *"So within these constraints, how can we help you?"*

It was a valuable starting point that concentrated minds. The session ended with a wish list, with a UK version of the Scottish Co-investment Fund firmly at the top. Within months, Ken Cooper, managing director of Capital for Enterprise, was pitching at the UK Business Angel Association winter workshop on 26 January 2011 for the creation of just such a joint equity fund.

Capital for Enterprise was one of several UK government bodies set up in 2009 to provide a range of financial support for SMEs. It was created as a non-departmental public body by BIS to deliver and manage capital and debt on behalf of the public and private sector. Its job was to stimulate growth in the laggard economy.

"The proposed co-investment fund recognises that business angels are the most significant source of early-stage capital in the sub-£1 million market of early-stage ventures and aims to leverage this potential," said Ken Cooper. "The fund would aim to act as a 'big business angel', sharing the risk with private investors, investing as a partner alongside angel networks and syndicates with a view to leveraging at least £2 angel investment alongside each £1 put in by the fund."

By March 2011, Capital for Enterprise was responsible for over £500 million of UK government commitments into equity funds. Alison Loudon, who had been connected with Archangels and knew Mike and Barry well, was one of the non-executive directors. Ken Cooper, who had initially been sceptical about co-investment funds, was won over and put in a worked-up bid for a £100 million fund to Vince Cable, the Business Secretary. In the end, it secured £50 million as the Angel CoFund, modelled on the Scottish Co-investment Fund. The fund was then launched in November and in May 2012 announced its first five investments, totalling £7.2 million.

"The Scottish Co-investment Fund is recognised

internationally as a model of best practice," said Sandy Finlayson. "This has been followed by the Angel CoFund and Archangels has been at the absolute heart of this process."

On Friday, 10 February 2012, the then Coalition Prime Minister David Cameron and Lord Young invited senior business angel figures to a breakfast panel discussion in Downing Street. Sandy Finlayson, David Grahame and John Waddell were present. The Prime Minister opened the meeting:

> *"First of all, I don't want to sound like Lord Kitchener, but your country needs you, really needs you," he said. "We clearly have a challenge getting economic growth going in our country and we have a massive challenge rebalancing our economy and providing sustainable private sector jobs."*

But the Prime Minister's second point was proper recognition of how far business angels had come since Mike and Barry began 20 years earlier:

> *"I hope that it's recognised that the government is trying to do what it can to help angels and business investment. The EIS scheme and the extension of it, allowing a million pounds to be invested each year, having the income tax advantages of it that we put in place, having the new seed funding arrangements as well. Basically, we've taken your ideas and we've put them straight into the budget. So, we're keen that we do everything we can to publicise what's already been done."*

"I was impressed. He clearly understood what we did and its importance to the UK economy," said John.

"After his introduction, he took hard, detailed questions for 15 minutes," said Sandy. "It wasn't just that he was in command of his brief, he knew about angel investment. We were being taken seriously and asked for our views."

David Cameron obviously struck a chord. Before taking the questions and handing the session over to Lord Young, Cameron concluded:

> *"It's nice to be an angel, isn't it? But it really means something because it means you are sitting on the shoulders and standing behind the people that you're helping. And you're not just helping them with money, you're helping them with advice. And I do think that's going to be particularly important at this stage of the economic cycle where lots of people have dreams and ideas of new businesses and actually the rate of new business formation is very great."*

The UK Prime Minister wasn't the only one impressed. Scotland's then First Minister Alex Salmond also recognised the world-leading significance of Archangels and the creation of syndicates at a special 20th anniversary event in Edinburgh Castle in November 2012, where Barry and Mike were both acknowledged as the founders of *"perhaps the oldest angel syndicate in the world"*. (Wiltbank USA)

9

COLLABORATION IS GOOD

Collaboration with other partners is at the heart of Archangels' success. Archangels' key partner is the Scottish Investment Bank, a publicly funded organisation that co-invests alongside Archangels and other syndicates. This model has been unique to Scotland and is now being embraced throughout the UK and is admired abroad.

Kerry Sharp, Investment Director of the Scottish Investment Bank, which oversees the Scottish Co-investment Fund, said there has been a successful evolution of the public and private sectors working hand-in-glove.

"In our minds, one of the benefits is not just the syndicate investor's cash, but their business expertise; people such as Barry and Mike who have first-class business experience that they can share. John Waddell and his team work very closely with us on an almost day-to-day basis," said Kerry.

"We carry out a lot of diligence on the partners to the Co-investment Fund to make sure we are comfortable. After all, this is tax-payers' money we are investing. Once we have invested in a company, we review the angel partners and investment syndicates and keep a close eye on developments.

"When we are comfortable with this, we leave the angel investor to do the diligence on the actual start-up company. Within certain parameters, we let the angels make the investment decision. As long as they satisfy the European criteria, we will invest on the back of that."

A significant amount of ERDF money underpins the various funds, and it comes with various criteria and certain exclusions attached, such as the fact that angels cannot fund the retail sector.

"From the public sector side, the process is really slick and very quick and inexpensive," said Pat McHugh, one of the architects of the Co-investment Fund. "When business angels are looking for something from us, we turn it around in a couple of days. At the beginning, the private sector partners were reticent about dealing with the public sector; their investment experience had been that working with the public sector takes too long, but one of the big pluses of the Co-investment Fund has been its speed of decision-making: they make the decision and look to us for a quick eligibility decision and, two or three days later, they get it."

Another type of collaboration for Archangels has been its long-term support for larger venture funds. In February 2005 Sandy Finlayson was asked by Peter Shakeshaft to join a conference call for a new outfit. It turned out to be opportune and Sandy became involved in setting up Seraphim Capital in August 2005.

"I spent 18 months on these monthly conference calls," he said. "This was the UK's first Enterprise Capital Fund. The idea was to get ten business angel syndicates to sign up. In the end, we got nine," he said.

The nine are Archangels, GLE Growth Capital, Pi Capital, The Summit Group, New Vantage Group, Focus Enterprise Inc, Entrust, Advantage Business Angels and Seraphim. This gives the Scottish syndicate a truly global perspective and interest, with John Waddell on the advisory board.

Each was to sign up to place £1 million into a pot, with one of the angels putting in £2 million, and the UK government was to match it, thus amassing a £20 million fund. Sandy and his team ended up representing Seraphim Capital, with Archangels pledging £1 million. Sandy handled the first of three Enterprise Capital Funds.

Among the key connections on Seraphim's advisory board have been Anthony Clarke, chairman of the British Business Angels Association since 2004, and the President of EBAN (European Business Angel Network). Anthony is a leading figure in the European angel community and is involved with London Business Angels and London Seed Capital. Also on the board is John May, recognised as a founding father of the concept of structured angel investment. He has been involved with the movement in the United States since the early 1990s and was a founding member of the Angel Capital Association, which consists of 200 groups across America. Seraphim managed to source £1 million of American angel investment after David Grahame introduced Anthony to John May and his successor, John Houston, of the Angel Capital Association in the USA.

John Waddell also cites Archangels' continuing collaboration with Amadeus Capital Partners in the Amadeus & Angels Seed Fund, which, among other things, provided seed funding for a Stirling University software spin-out called oneDrum, based in the university's Innovation Park. OneDrum allows co-authors to work on Microsoft Office documents in real-time, enabling teams to work together more easily. The company raised $2 million in funding from Amadeus, the UK Technology Strategy Board and Scottish Enterprise. Alex van Someren worked on the deal on behalf of Amadeus and it was sold to Yammer in April 2012 for an undisclosed figure.

Meanwhile, Scotland's syndicates have continued to work closely through LINC Scotland, which now represents Archangels and 19 other groups at government level in Edinburgh, London and Brussels, and is a member of the European Business Angels Association.

"It all works well on a collaborative basis and David Grahame must take a lot of credit for the way that he co-ordinated this through his LINC Scotland connection," said Peter Shakeshaft.

"It was never a cut-throat competitive scene," said David. "At a personal level there is rivalry, but the angel groups would not fight each other for deals. It was always highly collaborative; they would phone each other informally and they would share deals. This is how we managed to get syndicating between the groups."

10

A Lesson for the Future

The lingering recession in 2012 brought the work of Archangels into sharp focus. Politicians of almost every hue woke up to the fact that supporting the country's wealth creators is the only way to build a sustainable economy that supports a massive welfare system and a universal health service.

"In a recession it is difficult to do business because of the lack of markets and the lack of finance from banks," said Cala Homes founder and Archangels' board member Geoff Ball. "However, Archangels is still supporting new businesses that can grow incrementally and there is equity in the Archangels 'club' to feed those businesses. It is something that was active and vigorous when everything else was slowing down in the recession."

The lesson for the future is that angel investing syndicates have a vital part to play in Britain and in Scotland. The UK government is interested in 'investor appetite' and is keen to expand the number of people using EIS tax relief to encourage more business. There are 10,000 EIS investors in the UK and 300,000 households that pay 45% tax, so more people should be involved.

The EIS regime, which the UK government has delivered to encourage growth, remains a simple mechanism and at the core to what Archangels does.

"If an individual invests in an appropriately qualifying company – and that's not difficult because there are only a few exceptions, such as retail, property or financial services – when you invest, you receive tax relief," said Barry.

Archangels is now an influential part of a strongly interconnected system of finance for developing business. This comprises a network of professional advisers able to help growing firms and move up the funding 'escalator' as they require larger amounts of money.

"It is quite clear that governments in Holyrood and in Westminster realise that start-up businesses is where the growth in employment is coming from," said John Waddell.

Archangels has now been at the forefront of early-stage investing in Scotland for a quarter of a century. Today it is a tight-knit professional operation with a full-time executive team. A long-term owner of businesses with no specific investment time horizons, Archangels operates outwith the traditional fundraising and divestment cycles that can lead to short-term decision-making. The average length of time it has invested in companies in its current active portfolio is 7.5 years and the initial investment in the oldest company, Oregon Timber Frame, was made 19 years ago.

The average cash returned to Archangels investors in the companies that achieved successful exits was 2.7 times.

"Archangels is a brand and important for Scotland; it is admired internationally," said John. "We are the guys at the tiller now. It is our responsibility to be running the biggest angel group in Scotland, and possibly the UK and Western Europe. And the oldest business angel group in the world. We have a big responsibility to our investors and I believe we have big responsibilities to maintain this because it is an important part of developing the Scottish economy."

Archangels has been instrumental in encouraging others to take up the mantle of angel investing, demonstrating how well it can work. A report in October 2012 on the financing of business innovation in Scotland by the Royal Society of Edinburgh[1] said:

"The informal investment or business angel community in Scotland is among the most highly developed and structured in Europe."

The report authors credit Scotland's angel community with coming to the rescue in the early-stage capital market after the dotcom collapse in the early 2000s, when the venture capitalists left the field – a key part of Archangels' history. The report stated:

---

1 – 'The Financing of Business Innovation in Scotland,' Royal Society of Edinburgh Business Innovation Forum, October 2012.

"There has been a progressive transition over the past 10 or 15 years from the environment in which individuals or small groups made investments based on personal contact with entrepreneurs to a much more organised and less informal infrastructure."

Again, this could have been written specifically to refer to Archangels:

"The majority of angel investment is now undertaken by managed syndicates, typically ranging in size from a few dozen to around a hundred individuals."

And while processes and procedures vary among Scotland's syndicates, they generally involve a preliminary evaluation of the investment by a professional investment manager or a 'gatekeeper'. This report also raised an important issue: the timescale of each investment:

"The increasing organisation and structure around angel investment has led to a progressively more analytical approach, with more attention being given to performance across syndicate portfolios. It has also led, particularly in the current environment, to a more intense focus on outcomes and timescales."

John Waddell was among the participants at the Royal Society forum which stated that "creation of wealth by entrepreneurial churn" is capable of significant economic impact. But the economic cycle plays its part too. For John, one of the biggest years for investment was 2009, with the syndicate raising £12 million, yet all of it was 'follow-on' money for companies, as the banking crisis made it particularly problematic for companies to access funding. There were no new deals that year. However, the market began to open up slightly in 2010.

"There was an exit drought, which began four of five years previously and got worse and worse. Then things began to pick up in 2010," he said.

Archangels' portfolio is big enough to command an influential position within the corridors of Scotland's political and economic agencies. Working in partnership, Archangels can help Scottish Enterprise, the national economic development agency, deliver its strategic priorities, one of which is focusing on 'growth companies', firms with the ability to deliver significant numbers of new jobs and impact on the economy. Scottish Enterprise is committed to simplifying the approach to supporting innovation and commercialisation, which chimes with many Archangels investors who have long held the view that excessive bureaucracy and red tape hold up commercial opportunities.

11

EXIT STAGE LEFT

As the oldest operating angel syndicate in the world, Archangels commissioned a report by the Hunter Centre for Entrepreneurship at Strathclyde Business School in 2015 – 'Archangels: Impact Evaluation of Activities, 1992–2015' by Dr Niall MacKenzie and Margaret Coughtrie. The report had two main objectives: to understand the economic impact of Archangels' investment activities during that period and to understand the wider, less tangible impact their activities have had within the Scottish economy.

During the period of the study, Archangels exited from 18 investee companies; of these, 12 remained in the UK, three moved abroad and three failed.

These 18 exits represented 22.5% of Archangels' total investments since inception by number, on which they created a value almost three times greater than the capital investment. Some £37 million of original investment had generated an additional wealth of over £60 million. Even after netting off the losses of the failures, the Archangels members generated around £48 million of additional return over their capital investment.

The report stated that, from an economic development perspective, the continued operation of the companies developed and then sold by Archangels in Scotland has clear benefits, and although the revenues generated and net jobs created post-sale are not directly attributable to Archangels, there is a strong case to be made that Archangels helped establish these companies in Scotland and contributed towards their continued presence and the ensuing economic benefits.

Archangels has never forced a sale on an unwilling management – and all of its exits have been fully endorsed by the founders. Its objective is to be in a position where it is able to provide funding for investee companies through to a profitable sale or float, but it can take years to prepare a piece of technology to the point of commercialisation and years more to achieve market penetration. Archangels actively works with its companies, where appropriate, to plan for exits and to consider the exit landscape.

The syndicate has worked on a number of trade sales over the years and has developed, together with lawyers Dickson Minto, an exit protocol that ensures consistency of approach. It has developed a standard set of documents from an initial non-disclosure agreement and sale process letters through to a standard-form sale and purchase agreement.

The period 2010–2015 yielded the highest frequency of exits for Archangels in its history, with interest often from overseas. Three sales alone recouped over £50 million, a bonus for Scottish Enterprise, which was able, through the exits, to recoup half the money it had invested via the Scottish Co-investment Fund – still with another 19 co-investments in place with Archangels.

Mpathy, Lab901, Crombie Anderson, Data Discoveries and Vitrology were all let loose from the portfolio. Mpathy, Lab901 and Vitrology are all life science companies that have recycled money back into Archangels and subsequently encouraged the syndicate members to reinvest.

Mpathy was sold to Danish medical healthcare product manufacturer Coloplast in a £22 million deal in November 2010, following the original investment by Archangels in 2003. Archangel investors, who invested almost £5.6 million into Mpathy, received about £11.8 million from the sale, while Scottish Enterprise, a joint investor through the Scottish Co-investment Fund, received about £4.2 million for its original £2 million investment. It was the exit from Mpathy that enabled Archangels to provide financial support to Touch Bionics.

"The members love exits because they want to do more investing," said Mary Jane Brouwers, one of the Archangels' investment executives. "But a lot of people are doing this as part of a wealth management strategy and they will have a budget for this type of investment, so unless they get an exit, they have spent their pot."

"Mpathy and Lab901 have been big for Archangels investors," said Gavin Gemmell. "Between us, we put a lot of money into those. Whether you make a profit or not, a big sum of money is coming back into your bank account. It is a huge relief and great for morale."

Data Discoveries had been a source of dividends for Archangels investors for a number of years, with the syndicate already having its initial investment paid back five times through dividends. The IRR (internal rate of return) of Data Discoveries is one of the best by Archangels, because the trade exit was simply a bonus. Data Discoveries was just breaking even, having already returned cash to investors through dividends and a capital restructuring, when it was bought by the GB Group, an identity management business, for £830,000 in June 2011. The original investment by Archangels was made in 1995.

Eric Young was less satisfied with the outcome of Lab901. Life had been looking brighter for Lab901, which had been bobbing along since 2001 with Archangels' support. Agilent Technologies, based in Santa Clara, was reported to be eyeing up the Edinburgh company, which had developed and marketed a TapeStation benchtop electrophoresis instrument and ScreenTape plastic-based consumables, which were highly regarded by biopharma researchers, R&D labs and quality-control institutions. Agilent sought to address the global demand for increasing automation of DNA and protein analysis.

Agilent was a massive company, employing 18,500 people around the globe, and a world leader in measurement, chemical analysis, biotechnology, life sciences and communications. By comparison, Lab901 employed 45 people. It was led by Joel Fearnley, the chief executive officer. Patrick Kaltenbach, a vice president of Agilent, recognised Lab901 as having outstanding technology and a talented team and wanted Joel and his colleagues to join Agilent's own electrophoresis system.

"Lab901 was not a winner, it was a tragedy in that it took too much money from us before it hit revenue and went on too long," said Eric. "Whether that was board, management or us as Archangels, collectively, we spent too much. It should have been a great success story, and in some ways it is, because it is still a Scottish-based business employing lots of people and developing technology, but, for me, we should have made a lot of money out of it, considering the energy we put into it."

Gavin sympathises with Eric's view but notes that some investors did better than others, depending on their entry point and the pricing of their support.

"Depending on where and when you put your money in, there were better returns," he said. "If you invested all the way through, following your money, you made a small profit. People who put money in the last two investment rounds made profits, and those who put money in at the start made profits, but those who invested in rounds two, three, four and five lost money."

Lab901 was bought by Agilent Technologies in February 2011 for an undisclosed sum.

Archangels has continued to enjoy a number of successful exits in recent years, chiefly by way of trade sale. Flexitricity was sold to Alpiq, a company listed in Geneva, in April 2014. The original investment by Archangels was made in 2005. The first open-market system allowing electricity customers to participate directly in balancing supply and demand in the electricity system, Flexitricity uses advanced networking technology linked to a number of existing standby generators and electricity consuming processes. By starting generators and stopping consumption during periods of stress in the electricity system, it helps keep the system secure and reduces carbon dioxide emissions associated with electricity generation.

February 2015 yielded the £259.3 million purchase of Archangels' first investment, Optos by Nikon, while, that August, Dundee life sciences business CXR Biosciences was sold by its shareholders to Manchester-based Concept Life Sciences with all 33 CXR staff, including the management team, joining the Concept Life Sciences Group.

"This move reflects Archangels' approach of investing early, providing support and further investment to allow our companies to grow and exiting at a mutually advantageous opportunity once they reach maturity," said Niki McKenzie, investment director at Archangels

Then, in November 2015, Bloxx, the Livingston-based web security specialist, was sold for an undisclosed sum to US technology group Akamai.

"We are proud that Archangels has been able to support Bloxx from an early stage to become the significant player that it is today, helping to protect email and internet users across the globe," said McKenzie. "We are confident that the business will thrive as part of Akamai, whose world-leading credentials in content delivery are second to none."

Bloxx, which employs 55 people at its offices in Livingston and Newton, Massachusetts, was founded in 1999 and provides web and email filtering for medium-sized and large organisations in education, business and the public sectors, helping to protect 800 million devices around the world. NASDAQ-listed Akamai said the acquisition of Bloxx and its SWG technology would complement its cloud security strategy for protecting businesses against internet risks.

In April 2016, Touch Bionics, the developer and manufacturer of world-leading upper limb prosthetic technologies, was sold to Össur Hf, the Iceland-based provider of prosthetic, bracing and support solutions, for £27.5 million.

Touch Bionics was the first company to be spun out of the NHS in Scotland when it was founded in 2003. At the time of its sale, it employed over 120 people from its operations in Scotland, Germany and the USA.

Touch Bionics represents only the latest in a remarkable period of exit activity in Archangels' history, and that activity shows no signs of abating any time soon.

"The broad point about exiting from companies is that it is bloody difficult," said John Waddell. "If you've not actually had to do it, then most people haven't a clue how hard it is. You need to understand all the technical stuff, all the stuff about employment law and money, warranties and indemnities in different jurisdictions; but you also need to be a social worker and a psychologist because mostly it's about people's feelings.

"It's all about culture, integration and relationships – and it's hard to manage. People who haven't done it very often tend to get worked up about all the wrong things."

12

BLEEDING EDGE MONEY

The report by the Hunter Centre for Entrepreneurship at Strathclyde Business School in 2015 revealed that, since Archangels was formed, its investors had invested £95 million of cash in 80 companies. Around £110 million of cash had been returned by the date of the report as exit proceeds or dividends. There were 23 active companies on the books, three dormant companies and 35 that had failed. There had been three IPOs, one MBO and 15 trade sales.

Of that total cash investment of £95 million across Archangels' portfolio since inception, £36.6 million was invested in companies where Archangels investors had successfully exited, returning £98.6 million of value. A further £41.3 million had been invested in the current active portfolio of 23 companies and, based on its previous track record, Archangels would expect to return a multiple of that cash investment to investors.

Only £13.6 million, or roughly 15% of the total cash invested by Archangels since inception, had been invested in companies that subsequently failed, although the failure rate in terms of the number of companies in the portfolio was 44%.

Archangels has a wide network of stakeholders and the executive team taps into the knowledge in this network to identify and manage the wide-ranging challenges of high-risk early-stage investing. Very early-stage investment is inherently risky and requires the level of specialisation and experience that Archangels has developed in order to be successful.

While early-stage companies have great potential strengths, they also have great vulnerabilities in terms of timing, unexpected market shifts and technological challenge. Things do not always go according to plan.

Timing delays were an issue for NCTech, for example. NCTech's iSTAR, the world's fastest and first fully automatic, 50 megapixel, 360-degree HDR camera, was originally developed for the military and police, but the iSTAR has multiple applications: from covert operations and police reporting of crime scenes to 3D laser documentation and asset management for the engineering and heritage sectors. There has been significant interest in the product from potential customers around the world but the long sales cycle meant that the company required an injection of working capital to ensure that momentum was not lost. Archangels understood this and the network was able to respond and invest.

Following its investment from Archangels, NCTech was able to recruit additional sector expertise to its team. Archangels works very closely with portfolio company executives to identify skills gaps and development opportunities at board and senior management levels.

Archangels originally invested in NCTech in 2011. Since initial funding, the export market for NCTech's products has grown significantly. In 2012, export sales were negligible, whereas, by 2015, NCTech's export sales amounted to 64% of total sales. The company's product attracts interest from around the world and it has achieved international expansion via website activity, building relationships with worldwide reseller networks and attending international trade exhibitions.

While Archangels will lead almost all funding rounds in which it participates, the financial strength and track record of the syndicate has allowed it to attract a number of co-investors, who invest alongside it, thereby leveraging the funding ability.

Its key partner is Scottish Enterprise, through SCIF, which has invested around £19 million in its active portfolio. Additional co-investment partners include other business angel syndicates such as TRI Cap and Barwell, but also venture capital and traditional debt sources. For example, in 2013, Archangels instigated a £3.25 million funding round for Lux Assure, bringing in ConocoPhillips, Statoil Technology Invest as well as the Scottish Investment Bank, demonstrating its ability to successfully co-invest with venture capitalist firms.

Over the past five years, the Archangels syndicate has invested an average of around £7 million per annum, most of which was put into follow-on rounds for existing portfolio companies.

The split of investment into new deals versus the current portfolio is driven by a large range of factors, such as the quality of new deals being presented, valuation aspirations, other available funding sources and strategic imperatives within the portfolio companies. However, on average, Archangels would expect 10–20% of its funding year-on-year to be deployed into new investments, with the balance being deployed in the existing portfolio. This split also reflects the importance placed by the syndicate on the requirement to fund or secure funding for its portfolio companies through all of their growth capital requirements.

"We never planned Archangels to be what it is now," said Barry. "We didn't have a strategy that we were going to grow it to the level that it is now; we just did what we did on an ongoing basis."

According to Archangels board member Geoff Ball, Archangels today is piggy-backing on the work that Mike and Barry have done.

"They have been at it for almost 25 years and invested in several different sectors," he said. "There is now a lot of domain expertise around Archangels; whether they are investors, past directors, customer directors or whatever else, there is always someone we can turn to if we want to do due diligence of a new investment."

Yet the contribution made by business angels to Scotland's economy remains less well known among the general public than it deserves. Research in Scotland, which tracked all the deals from 2003 to 2008, demonstrated that "business angel investment significantly outweighed institutional venture capital investment. Indeed, business angels are often the only source of external seed, start-up and growth finance available once businesses have exhausted personal and family sources and sources of 'soft money', such as the Prince's Youth Business Trust, proof of concept schemes, university challenges and SMART awards."[2]

Of course, the tax relief on investments is a significant factor that encourages most business angels to invest, but there is also a genuine interest in helping start-up businesses survive and thrive in Scotland, born out of a realisation that, if it is to prosper, Scotland needs to have more successful enterprises.

"VCs are far more kindred spirits in terms of what Archangels does now than when Barry and Mike started," said John Waddell. "However, Archangels doesn't receive funds and we don't write cheques; we facilitate the process which allows individuals to invest in young companies of their choice, directly to gain the EIS relief."

Where Archangels perhaps differs from VCs is that it often remains supportive if it takes longer than expected for a company in which it has invested to achieve the breakthrough.

---

2 – 'Developing Time Series Data on the Size and Scope of the UK Business Angel Market', Colin Mason and Richard Harrison, for Department of Business Enterprise & Regulatory Reform, May 2008.

"It is unlikely that a start-up will make its first sale within six months; it is more likely to take a year, and this needs to be funded," said Gavin Gemmell. "So long as we know people are working at it, are straight-forward and it looks as though there is still a prospect, we will keep supporting them. But we are clearer now that this will mean they will own less of the company. They will be diluted. We've become tougher about insisting on sticking to the business plan, because the pricing of the next round of funding will depend on this.

"We should be proud of what we have done. We have never wavered from the path of investing in new starts and providing development capital in new companies that don't have any turnover. Mike calls it 'bleeding edge money', because we don't know that their product will work, let alone sell. Many others who have started off doing something similar to what we do have quickly moved upscale to less risky and more established business, because losing money is easy."

13

THE HALO EFFECT

A recent study by lawyers Harper Macleod found that angel investors are disproportionately prominent in Scotland given the higher concentrations of wealth elsewhere in the world. In 2013 they provided over £27 million of investment in Scottish start-ups, dispensing cash in packages in the region of £20,000–£750,000. Research by the export and investment agency Scottish Development International (SDI) claims that Scotland has «more business angel investment per head of population than any other country in Europe».

And research into the risk capital market in Scotland 2014, published in December 2015 by Scottish Enterprise and Young Company Finance, revealed that angel investing continues to be a major part of the early-stage investment environment in Scotland. Reporting by financial year, LINC recorded all-time-high investment figures for 2014–2015, with 108 investments amounting to £43.2 million – in itself an 84% increase over the previous year. The amounts invested by business angels themselves showed the most dramatic increase: 76% above the previous financial year. This increase in investment levels is by no means restricted to follow-on investments in portfolio companies. Indeed, investments in new companies increased by over 100% to a level well in excess of the previous high point in 2013.

In February 2015 Archangels reported one of its strongest years for investing in Scottish technology and life sciences businesses, having arranged funding of £12.2 million for 14 companies in the previous year. That sum comprised £7.5 million from Archangels investors, with a further £3.5 million of co-investment from Scottish Enterprise and £1.2 million from other partners.

Its biggest single investment was £2.5 million in Touch Bionics, while, at the other end of the scale, the syndicate also invested £100,000 in Cytomos, an Edinburgh firm that uses electronics to analyse cells, underlining Archangels' appetite for investing in early-stage, higher-risk ventures.

Investors in the Archangels portfolio saw returns from disposals and dividends of £17.3 million in 2014, with £11.2 million going to Archangels members.

"This was one of Archangels' strongest years and, against a background of crowdfunders and other early-stage investors entering the market, the traditional investment model, pioneered by Archangels, is going from strength to strength," said John Waddell.

In June 2015 John announced his intention to step down as chief executive of Archangels in October, handing over the day-to-day operations to chief operating officer David Ovens, an experienced corporate financier who had worked for Samuel Montagu & Company, Noble Grossart and Noble & Company, before setting up Invercap, a corporate advisory boutique based in Edinburgh. John remains active in a consultancy role and as a director in some of the companies in which the syndicate members have invested.

That same month, *Scottish Business Insider* reported that Scotland had at least 1,100 business angels who invest their own money mainly in Scottish-based companies, but also elsewhere in the UK. The number may actually be three times that, according to David Grahame of LINC Scotland. The amount of money invested in companies by business angels is substantial. Over the past 15 years, members of LINC have invested £283 million in 531 companies. Some £200 million of that total was invested in the past decade.

Archangels' economic impact remains at the core of its philosophy. The syndicate has created more than 3,000 jobs since its creation in 1992 and the wider economic impact of its investment, mentoring and management support activities was the subject of the Hunter Centre for Entrepreneurship study mentioned earlier – which saw Dr Niall MacKenzie and Margaret Coughtrie examine the economic impact of Archangels and the companies in which it has invested in Scotland.

Welcoming delegates to an event at the University of Strathclyde Technology and Innovation Centre on Friday,

4 September 2015 to present the study's findings, Eleanor Shaw, head of the Hunter Centre for Entrepreneurship and Vice Dean, Enterprise and Knowledge Exchange, announced that the event was about acknowledging the impact that Archangels has had on innovation and the effect that has had on the Scottish economy.

Congratulating Dr MacKenzie and Margaret Coughtrie for their study, Mike Rutterford took the opportunity to thank Martin Hughes, a visiting professor at the University of Strathclyde, whom he described as an "unsung hero" and the "midwife" of the creation of the Scottish Co-investment Fund.

"Barry and I really didn't know what we were doing when we set up Archangels," reflected Mike. "We had no business plan and if we were to approach Archangels for funding today, we wouldn't invest in ourselves!"

He emphasised that Archangels is not one company but an agglomeration of around 80 businesses and that its job is to build around the embryo of a company over a period so that it becomes a standalone entity in its own right.

"One of the unforeseen benefits of Archangels' activities is the good that it has achieved for mankind," he said.

"One of our companies, Reactec, has developed technology that defends employees and employers from white finger disease, the third most common industrial injury in the UK. People can now avoid this irreversible disease.

"And Touch Bionics has transformed the lives of many people who have lost a hand or an arm, while with

Optos, not only have we saved people's sight, we know we've saved people's lives. I remember being at an Optos board meeting many years ago when we found that one of our optometrists in the USA had just acquired the system, done some imaging on friends and family and, as a result, by happenstance, identified that his daughter had a tumour on the brain and she was rushed to hospital. Several years later the company received a letter from this girl, thanking us for saving her life. She had made a full recovery.

"That for me is like hitting the jackpot and getting three cherries in a row on the one-arm bandit: we have fun, we make a bundle of money and we do good for mankind."

John Waddell then read out a note on behalf of the absent Barry Sealey.

"I'm very proud of Archangels' achievements," he said. "It is always particularly satisfying to see new ventures created and, in many cases, succeed. It is very pleasing to me that governments are recognising the importance of new companies and their role in building new technologies as a contribution to growing the economy.

"In that context, I value the help given through fiscal incentives and such schemes as the Co-investment Fund. What is important, however, is not just the money invested, but the wide range of help and support that is provided by Archangels alongside the cash. I feel sure that the angel movement can and will continue to provide an essential stimulus for growth within Scotland and throughout the UK."

Picking up on Mike's earlier aside that, when he and Barry had formed Archangels, they didn't really know what they were doing, Finance Secretary John Swinney suggested that this comment revealed an important part of the story of what Archangels has delivered in Scotland, namely "to cut new ground and to lead from the front and to get out there and do something that wasn't being done in the marketplace at that time and do it very successfully and in a fashion which has encouraged a whole range of other angel syndicates to come together".

The Finance Secretary went on to say that one of the great strengths of what Archangels has done for Scotland has been to force the public sector to engage as productively and constructively as itself in trying to find ways of supporting the development of new companies within the economy.

"The Scottish Co-investment Fund, established by Scottish Enterprise, has, over the last 12 years, encouraged and motivated by the partnership with Archangels, delivered some of that very meaningful support to new-start ventures within Scotland and has been an extremely positive intervention which has clearly had a very significant impact on the business support landscape within Scotland," he said.

"Organisations like Archangels can have the effect of prompting innovative policies within Scotland to make sure that we have the right interventions in place to support our wider objectives of improving and strengthening the business economy within Scotland."

Referencing 'Scotland Can Do', the Scottish government's shared statement of intent towards becoming a world-leading entrepreneurial and innovative nation, Mr Swinney expressed gratitude for the contribution made by Archangels over the years in informing that wider debate and on focusing the interventions that the government makes today.

"I was involved in a conversation recently with Barry about taking the principle of investing, of having fun, of doing good things, and identifying how the angel community can invest in the emergence of social enterprises within Scotland," he said.

"This was something that Barry made a profound and passionate contribution to and it was yet another example of how a good, wise, thoughtful concept is now being developed in another way in another space to have a more profound impact on the people of Scotland. That's something that I think we should be immensely proud of as a country, so to Mike and Barry, Archangels and everybody in the angel community, a warm word of thanks from the Scottish government for your impact on changing the business climate in Scotland. Scotland is the better for that and we're very grateful to you for demonstrating that leadership and that inspiration."

Introducing the findings of the economic study itself, Niall MacKenzie commented that the support available for high-growth-potential technology companies had come a long way since 1992, when Archangels was established.

"Back then there was a very different economic landscape in Scotland – a landscape where the staple industries of oil, steel and shipbuilding were declining and what we saw were two very entrepreneurial individuals in Mike Rutterford and Barry Sealey getting together and saying 'we can make a difference. We've made our money, we've done well out of Scotland, let's see what we can do to give back,'" he said.

"Archangels then grew to a syndicate with over 200 historic investors and a current pool of about 70 investors with an investment management team managing much of the activities. It has invested over £90 million in 80 early-stage, high-risk companies.

"Underpinning all this, there should be a recognition that they don't have to do this. Angel investors and Archangels are under no obligation to undertake these activities. Rather, they choose to do it because they feel they can do something that makes a difference. So when we consider these economic impacts – which are substantial – it's worth reminding ourselves that these are private individual initiatives which have come together and made a substantial difference to Scottish early-stage risk capital and Scottish economic development."

The report estimated that Archangels had created almost 3,000 jobs since its formation. While many of the companies involved were early stage, and often pre-revenue, they didn't pay particularly well at the outset but, over time, Archangels' companies create value and jobs that pay in excess of the average Scottish salary.

It was estimated that the total turnover created by Archangels from 1992 till 2015 was between £1.31 billion and £1.87 billion – a number MacKenzie commented he was "surprised and delighted in equal measure to find".

And it was estimated that, for every £1.00 invested by Archangels, between £14.34 and £20.04 was generated, which compared to $6.23 generated for every $1.00 invested by US venture capital companies.

"That number speaks volumes about the quality of investments that Archangels makes and the quality of the activities that it undertakes," suggested MacKenzie.

"Archangels has been doing this for a long time and is able to leverage investment and the knowledge and the networks and the capital that it has effectively into growth for Scottish companies."

The research revealed that Archangels generates a GVA (gross value added) figure of £1.5 million per annum per company invested in, which compares to a GVA of £1.13 million per annum for other Scottish Co-investment Fund partner investors. MacKenzie attributes Archangels' superior GVA to its "longevity, experience, expertise and willingness to engage in what are often high-risk companies".

According to MacKenzie, Archangels has always had an open innovation policy that encouraged shared learning and shared documentation.

"It played other smaller investors into its deals and took an open arms policy to help grow the market and help establish angel investment in Scotland," he said. "The establishment of the Scottish Co-investment Fund saw growth in angel activity from 2003 onwards and

Archangels had a very important role to play within that."

With regard to the performance of Archangels' portfolio, MacKenzie observed that "failures are an unavoidable part of angel investment" and that some 44% of Archangels' investments had failed, representing "only" 15% of the money invested, or £13.6 million.

The research showed that Archangels' average investment period for failed companies was 3.7 years, which, suggested MacKenzie, showed that it spots failures early.

"Archangels is a very patient investor," he said, adding, "25% of the active portfolio is pre-revenue at any one time and the average investment period over the whole portfolio is six years, and eight years for sold companies. That shows that Archangels will take time to build a company."

Since its formation, Archangels has invested £36.6 million in exited companies, which returned over £100 million of value to investors. Archangels' ten-year return to 2014 was 21%, which compared with a British Venture Capital Association return of 15%, indicating that Archangels is achieving impressive returns.

Eighteen of Archangels' investee companies have been exited. Twelve remain in the UK, three have relocated overseas and three have been dissolved. "That shows that Archangels creates value in Scotland, which stays, largely, in Scotland," said MacKenzie. "Of the 12 companies remaining in the UK, three moved down south and nine stayed in Scotland, an impressive return in terms of the value that Archangels adds to economic development in Scotland."

Stating that early-stage investment is of fundamental importance to helping companies grow and realise their potential, MacKenzie said that Archangels has played a critical role in developing some of Scotland's brightest companies and entrepreneurial culture.

The report confirmed that Archangels continues to support pre-revenue companies – 25% of its active portfolio over the period has typically comprised high-risk technology investments that do not generate revenue. It also showed that Archangels offers more than just financial support – it has helped grow the Scottish business angel market through the sharing of operational learning with other angel groups and it supports investee companies by opening up access to its networks of professional and other contacts, thereby helping to add value to the companies and the wider Scottish economy.

It cited research which suggested that firms value hands-on, relational support from peers or role models, particularly if this is tailored to their specific strategic and management challenges, and suggested that Archangels has become well-known for taking exactly this approach to its investments in high-growth-potential Scottish companies.

Barry Sealey describes it as "getting your arms around a company" to help it grow.

As revealed in the report, Archangels typically leads all funding rounds in which it participates and leverages the financial strength and track record of its syndicate to bring in other investors where appropriate, in what has been termed 'bundled investment'. In recent years this has resulted in several of its companies benefiting from the involvement of other angel groups such as TRI Cap and Barwell, as well as single investors, and large organisations including Amadeus, 3i, ConocoPhillips, Statoil Technology Invest, Scottish Enterprise and the Scottish Investment Bank, bringing both financial benefits and global expertise to Scottish companies.

On the one hand, this spreads risk for all parties, but on the other, it encourages greater deal flow, plays in other angel groups and allows for access to greater networks of the social and reputational capital the investors hold for investee companies. As the report stated:

> *Archangels' ability to undertake deals of a higher average value is a critical part of both encouraging deal flow by virtue of Archangels being an active and willing investor, which encourages growth potential companies that finance is available, even where companies need a higher level of funding in order to achieve loftier growth ambitions.*

The report contains Barry Sealey's oft-repeated mantra that Archangels offer financing, as well as 'HELP' focused around getting companies market-ready, whether it is encouraging processual change within the company or bringing in external support and help in the form of non-executive directors or experienced executives, or leveraging wider social and industry contacts and reputations to help companies access new markets, products, services and financing.

Archangels took a decision early on to share learning with other angels and angel groups where appropriate in order to help grow the business angel market in Scotland. This decision was important for various reasons, including the fact that in the early 2000s a majority of business angels lacked experience of small business.

The report's authors noted that Archangels' position as a visible, committed investor that is willing to share its knowledge and experience in the angel process continues to be an important component in encouraging angel investment, entrepreneurial behaviour and significant levels of financial capital to support high-growth-potential Scottish firms. With the growth in the number of angel groups and deals being done in Scotland, Archangels has found itself in the position of being a grandee in the market – it is able to act as well as share its experiences with other angels, which in turn has had a halo effect of encouraging a greater entrepreneurial culture in Scotland.

By virtue of being first in the market in terms of organising itself, Archangels occupies an important place within the Scottish business angel landscape. From being a two-man partnership, the syndicate now has a large number of members and has formalised itself increasingly in terms of how it operates and the types of investments that it makes.

There is a large degree of trust and complementarity in how angels operate in Scotland that sees them compete, but not undermine each other. The open innovation approach taken by Archangels from an early stage has helped facilitate the wider growth of angel investing in Scotland and helped supply capital in an area of the market in which it is difficult for policymakers to engage due to the high risk of failure and the need to protect public monies.

A further aspect to Archangels' patient approach is its willingness to support businesses that are not yet producing revenue. No profit means no return to providers of financial capital. Six of the 14 companies within which Archangels has invested in the past decade are still pre-revenue, with one of those companies having been in the portfolio for more than 10 years. Pre-revenue companies have typically comprised around 25% of Archangels' active portfolio throughout its period of investment.

According to the report's authors, it is clear from the analysis undertaken that Archangels continues to play a critical role in supporting high-growth-potential companies and helping grow and deepen the angel investment marketplace in Scotland. Archangels operates at a higher financial level than the rest of the visible angel market in Scotland and provides support to companies, policymakers and other angel groups as well as a willingness to engage across a variety of different issues.

As Scotland's oldest angel syndicate, Archangels has been a vital factor in the substantial growth in angel investing in the country and enjoys a strong reputation among different stakeholders within the community. Its willingness to include other angels in deals, sharing information and learning, and with open lines of communication, has helped create the competitive collegiality that characterises the angel investment community in Scotland.

The report states:

> *The outcomes of our analysis of key measures of turnover generation, net employment created, average salary per job created over period of investment, and GVA contribution reveals that Archangels' impact in economic development terms is both substantial and far exceeds its pure financial investment, although it has successfully returned capital and provided capital uplift to its investors. Archangels continues to play a crucial role in supporting early stage companies in Scotland in line with national economic strategic priorities and has helped facilitate the growth and establishment of a number of new ventures through its blended approach of patience, finance and HELP.*

Archangels' early engagement in supporting early-stage, high-risk companies was key to helping persuade Scottish policymakers of the need to support angel investors in Scotland in order to ensure innovative companies were given every opportunity to survive, thrive and grow. This has resulted in the creation of a number of high-impact Scottish technology companies that are active in the global marketplace and contributing significantly to Scottish economic growth and the replication in other countries of what has become known as the 'Scottish Model' of public–private partnering in supporting early-stage, high-growth-potential companies in the move towards leveraging knowledge as a competitive asset. Archangels' pioneering angel activities have contributed in no small measure to creating the vibrant and enterprising Scotland we see today.

Kerry Sharp, head of the Scottish Investment Bank, noted that the report not only articulated the work that Archangels has done through its activities, but also demonstrated the beneficial impact of the partnership approach between the public and private sectors.

"When the Scottish Co-investment Fund made its first investment in 2003 we only had three co-investment partners on our books, Archangels being one," she said. "The market has evolved considerably since then, as has the Scottish Co-investment Fund, and Archangels has supported us throughout that evolution. Archangels remains one of the most active investors in the market, but also one of our most valued partners."

According to Sharp, Scotland is admired across the world for the pivotal role it has played in the development of angel investment.

"Angel investment is now part of the ecosystem; it is embedded in what we do in Scotland and that is something that's understood across the world," she said.

"This research shows the vital role that risk capital plays in growing economies. The numbers themselves are impressive, but it's not just the investment; it's the support that goes with it. The support that early-stage companies get, from Archangels, other investors, and from Scottish Enterprise, really does make an impact."

Commenting on the way that Archangels works with its companies, with the market and with Scottish Enterprise, Sharp described the syndicate as "a committed investor which works openly, honestly and is always willing to support others. I very much value the partnership we have with Archangels and look forward to continuing to work with them for a long time to come and to see that wider capital risk market really pushing forward with successes coming to Scotland on the back of that," she concluded.

Emphasising that Archangels is not just about providing capital, but about providing intelligent capital and supporting capital, David Ovens, Archangels' chief operating officer, said that the syndicate mentors entrepreneurs and adds value to their businesses.

"Scottish Enterprise is our most important partner and provides an undeniable source of finance to the early-stage funding market in Scotland," he said.

David noted that all of Archangels' investee companies are based in Scotland and the majority are in high-growth technology businesses employing highly skilled people.

"Companies like Touch Bionics, NCTech, Administrate, Zone Fox and others within our portfolio are delivering exciting, disruptive technology with worldwide markets," he said. "Indeed, over 80% of our companies have significant export sales."

While stating that Archangels was the pioneer of

the business angel market in Scotland in 1992, David suggested that, with the establishment of LINC Scotland and SCIF, an industry has emerged within Scotland that is of vital importance to the growth of the Scottish economy.

"Archangels has maintained a consistent investment approach since it was formed – disruptive technology companies based in Scotland with export growth potential and strong management teams – and we align ourselves with management teams and support them through the journey of building their businesses," he said.

"We value the stability and consistency of approach we receive from Scottish Enterprise and the Scottish Co-investment Fund and we value the stability of the fiscal framework within which we operate. These are both fundamental to what we do."

According to David, one of the things that differentiates Archangels from other players in the market is that it has an investment team which adds value to the members by way of deep appraisal and rigorous due diligence, as well as by supporting management teams, understanding exit landscapes, managing the exit process, creating value for investors and making good use of its extensive network of industry experts.

Commenting on his decision to step down as CEO of Archangels after a decade in the post, John Waddell echoed Peter Shakeshaft's sentiments by describing the position as "the best job in Scotland" and drew an analogy to explain what working at Archangels had been like.

"Some years ago I was managing the acquisition of a

handmade brick company near Colchester which had a huge pugmill machine that ground up clay at one end and, at the other, a great big box where three men never stopped scooping up the clay as it came out of the ground, turning around and putting it on a pallet before bending down again and scooping out the clay again ... and it always struck me that, if they ever stopped, they would just disappear in a big pile of clay ... and that's what working at Archangels is like!" he said.

"There is never, ever nothing to do – and you're in danger of getting in a terrible mess if you don't keep up."

John wound up the formal aspect of the event by reflecting on a recent conversation with an entrepreneur-in-residence at UK Trade & Investment about the razzmatazz and excitement emerging about early-stage investing, what with the formation of the Seed Enterprise Investment Scheme (SEIS), the Silicon Roundabout, crowdfunding, *Dragon's Den* and other initiatives.

"He concluded the conversation with an interesting comment," recalled John. "He said, 'When all of that other stuff has disappeared, when there's no SEIS left, when all the crowdfunders have given up and gone home, Archangels will still be around doing ten or 15 deals a year for early-stage companies in Scotland.' And that's *exactly* what we'll be doing."

In March 2017, the outputs from the Strathclyde report were updated to reflect what had been achieved during Arch-angels' first quarter-century. The updated report found that for every £1 invested by Archangels, its portfolio companies have contributed an estimated £7.61–£9.51 of GVA to the Scottish economy. Archangels' companies are estimated to have generated turnover of at least £1.392 billion since 1992, representing £14.34 for every £1 invested. Impressively, the companies in which Archangels has invested are estimated to have created more than 3,550 jobs.

14

BEYOND JUST MONEY

The Scottish government report 'The Market for SME Finance in Scotland' published in August 2015 noted that Scotland's business angel investment activity is well established and organised and has played a key role in improving the availability of seed and early- stage investment up to £2 million. Tax relief (EIS and SEIS) is a major part of the angel space, providing a strong incentive for what is a risky activity, and Scottish public sector support has enabled activity in excess of other UK regions. For investments between £100,000 and £2 million, the most recent analysis revealed that business angels account for around 35% of total investment.

Over the past five years, angels and angel groups within the LINC Scotland trade body have invested between £14 million and £17 million per year. There is a need for increased amounts of follow-on investment before company exits are achieved, the time of which have lengthened considerably over recent years from an average of seven to ten years. This lack of recycling of returns limits the amount of investment available for new ventures.

The constant quest for improvement continues. The Scottish government recently established an Innovation Forum that recognises the strides already made and is seeking to capitalise on what has already been done. Government-funded agencies continue to make a difference. Interface brings together academics and businesses and Innovate UK has brought substantial non-dilutive funding to Scottish companies.

Privately funded initiatives, such as Entrepreneurial Spark and Codebase, have created exciting incubators for young companies, providing the benefit of mutual support, knowledge transfer and shared experience. The Saltire Foundation is working hard to create a cohort of skilled managers to run the businesses of the future in Scotland.

Foreign investors are taking an interest and have contributed to the creation of Scotland's two unicorns (private companies valued at more than $1 billion), FanDuel and Skyscanner. In addition, Epidarex, a life sciences VC, has set up and found funds and deals in Scotland, while Edinburgh University has recently increased the funds available to Old College Capital to invest mainly in spin-outs.

"The core of Archangeling is all about arranging, dealing, managing and administering investment. That bit of the Financial Services legislation has not really been updated," said Sandy Finlayson. "We've had to work incredibly hard to make it fit for purpose. Today Archangels has a structure which functions properly. Furthermore, it acts as an ever-green fund. Almost 25 years on, it is still there and still investing £9–10 million a year."

The angel investment market in Scotland continues to develop and evolve, aided by continuing support from the public sector.

"Year on year, we have continued to grow the Co-investment Fund, increasing the number of investment partners," said Jim McFarlane of Scottish Enterprise. "Along the way, we have also addressed the disparity of activity. It is well developed in the East Coast of Scotland but less developed in the West Coast and other parts of the country, which we are working on."

"The Co-investment Fund has been a huge help to us. Where they sign up as investment partners with people like us, they don't try to pick and choose the winners, as they did before, so they follow along with us," said Mike Rutterford. "They trust us because we take the money out of our own pockets and invest: that's the acid test.

"Yet the public sector could help more by giving young companies an opportunity to take on some of its contracts. Buy our products rather than give us a grant; it's the easiest way to fund companies."

Sandy agrees with Barry Sealey that, despite Archangels' increasing formalisation and sophistication over the years, its focus must remain rooted in real 'risk' capital.

"As an Archangels investor, you still have to be prepared to lose all your investment, but the methods we have developed professionalise the whole thing as far as we can," he said.

With that caveat, Alastair Salvesen encourages more high-net-worth individuals to step forward as Archangels and be prepared to take such a risk. Gavin Gemmell is in full agreement.

"We need to widen the group," he acknowledged. "We have a group of younger people who have done well from selling their businesses who have been joining. They are in their 40s, so when they are in their 50s, they might choose to spend more time on Archangels business."

As of March 2017, Archangels members have invested £103.5m in 83 companies and the syndicate has returned more than £125 million to its members through exits and dividends since its formation. Including extra capital that has been leveraged alongside its investment, Archangels has managed a total investment of £221 million since 1992.

David Ovens, Archangels' chief operating officer, said, "We continued to invest at record levels and, in doing so, support some of the most exciting technology companies in Scotland.

"We are particularly proud that our investment levels have increased in recent years, which can only be good for the Scottish economy, for jobs and for entrepreneurship in Scotland."

Reflecting on the evolution of Archangels since its formation almost a quarter of a century ago, Mike Rutterford acknowledged that Barry Sealey underlines the fact that Archangels has always been about more than money.

"You have to give a bit of yourself; pass on the lessons you've learned and offer some advice from your own experience. Some call us angels, well, maybe so, but, if so, we're angels that get our hands dirty," he said.

"Our philosophy is to really get stuck in and help companies at the coalface to realise their ambitions. Taking Optos as just one example, Barry and I derive a great quiet pleasure from the knowledge that we've played a part in the development of a technology that saves people's lives. We know we've helped save people's sight and it's gratifying to have been involved in creating world-beating technology that has benefited mankind. That's got to be good stuff; beyond just money."

Company Name	Status	Date of First Archangel Investment	Sector
Electronic Book Factory	Failed	Sep 1992	Software
Optos	IPO and subsequent sale	Oct 1992	Medical Equipment
Objective Software Technology	Trade Sale	Mar 1993	Software
Solcom Systems	Trade Sale	Mar 1993	Software
Replyline	Failed	Apr 1994	Specialized Consumer Services
KikaFlik	Failed	May 1994	Toys
Neatwork (International)	Failed	May 1994	Recreational Products
Key Radio Systems (Scotland)	Failed	Sep 1994	Telecommunications Equipment
Babbage Engineering	Failed	Feb 1995	Computer Services
Data Discoveries	Trade Sale	Oct 1995	Computer Services
Bio-medical Instrumentation	Failed	Mar 1996	Medical Equipment
Waterside Television	Failed	Sep 1996	Broadcasting & Entertainment
Libris Computing	Failed	Oct 1996	Software
AIM Technologies Europe	Failed	May 1997	Software
Alpha Solway	Trade Sale	July 1997	Software
Makar Productions	Failed	Oct 1997	Broadcasting & Entertainment
Sirius Seven Software	Dormant	Dec 1997	Software

Euroburo	Failed	Dec 1997	Business Support Services
Lifestar	Failed	Dec 1997	Business Training & Employment Agencies
Oregon Timber Frame	Active	Feb 1998	Heavy Construction
Crombie Anderson Associates	Trade Sale	Apr 1998	Business Support Services
Survey & Development Services	Failed	Dec 1998	Real Estate Services
Gencell	Failed	Aug 1999	Biotechnology
Infinite Data Storage	Failed	Feb 2000	Computer Services
Garplaid	Failed	Mar 2000	Software
The Internet Car Company	Failed	Mar 2000	Automobiles
Tissue Science Laboratories	IPO and subsequent sale	Mar 2000	Biotechnology
The Flower Company (UK)	Failed	May 2000	Specialty Retailers
Maximedia (Scotland)	Failed	July 2000	Computer Services
Internet Business Services	Failed	Aug 2000	Business Support Services
Multiverse Solutions	Failed	Sep 2000	Computer Services
Weathermac	Failed	Sep 2000	Industrial Suppliers
Arrayjet	Active	Feb 2001	Medical Equipment
Hanon Solutions	Trade Sale	Apr 2001	Software
White Dentalcare	Failed	May 2001	Healthcare Providers
Gyneideas	Trade Sale	Aug 2001	Medical Supplies
CXR Biosciences	Trade Sale	Dec 2001	Biotechnology
Amoebics	Failed	Apr 2002	Biotechnology

Stortext Group	Trade Sale	Apr 2002	Delivery Services
Bau.waus	Failed	May 2002	Food Products
Orkell	Failed	July 2002	Software
Lab901	Trade Sale	Sep 2002	Medical Equipment
Yaba	Failed	Oct 2002	Medical Supplies
Stem Cell Sciences	IPO	July 2003	Biotechnology
Lux Assure	Active	Oct 2003	Oil Equipment & Services
Mpathy Medical Devices	Trade Sale	Oct 2003	Medical Supplies
Adaptive Venture Managers	Failed	Nov 2003	Business Support Services
I-Dare Innovation	Failed	Dec 2003	Software
Touch Bionics	Trade Sale	Feb 2004	Medical Equipment
Earlsgate Holdings	Failed	Mar 2004	Software
Reactec	Active	Apr 2004	Electronic Equipment
Indigo Lighthouse Group	Active	June 2004	Delivery Services
Bloxx	Trade Sale	June 2004	Internet
Instant Group	Failed	July 2004	Software
Scalar Technologies	Failed	Nov 2004	Diversified Industrials
Blacket Research	Failed	Feb 2005	Software
Critiqom	Active	June 2005	Delivery Services
Adventi	Failed	July 2005	Computer Services
Sentient Medical	Active	Aug 2005	Medical Equipment
Flexitricity	Trade Sale	Nov 2005	Alternative Electricity

Trig Avionics	Active	June 2006	Aerospace
eoLogic	Failed	Aug 2006	Software
Iris-3D	Failed	Nov 2006	Computer Hardware
Vitrology	Trade Sale	Mar 2007	Biotechnology
Verisim	Failed	May 2007	Software
Powerphotonic	Active	Nov 2007	Diversified Industrials
Ateeda	Active	July 2008	Semiconductors
MGB Biopharma	Active	Feb 2010	Biotechnology
Vibio (UK)	Failed	May 2010	Internet
NetThings	Active	Aug 2010	Electronic Equipment
Airborne Energy	Failed	Sep 2010	Alternative Electricity
Administrate	Active	Dec 2010	Software
Xi Engineering Consultants	MBO	May 2011	Business Support Services
Fios Genomics	Active	July 2011	Biotechnology
NCTech	Active	Oct 2011	Electronic Equipment
Oxy-Gen Combustion	Trade Sale	Jan 2012	Conventional Electricity
Calcivis	Active	Aug 2012	Medical Equipment
Blackford Analysis	Active	Sep 2012	Software
Inquisitive Systems/ Zonefox	Active	Feb 2013	Software
Cytomos	Active	Dec 2014	Medical Equipment
JWEB	Active	Aug 2015	Biotechnology
Optoscribe	Active	May 2016	Telecommunications Equipment
Physiomedics	Active	Dec 2016	Healthcare Providers

ACKNOWLEDGEMENTS

Kenny Kemp

Thanks for the time and input of John Waddell, Mary Jane Brouwers, Barry Sealey, Mike Rutterford, June Rutterford, Sir Gerald Elliot, Sir Brian Souter, Dr Ian Sword, Geoff Ball, Robert Pattullo, Douglas Anderson, Anne Glover, Gavin Gemmell, Colin McGill, David Grahame, Sandy Finlayson, Stuart Hendry, Melanie Schwindt, Nelson Gray, Juliette Chapman, Ian Stevens, Keith Howell, Stephane Sallmard, Lynne Cadenhead, Pat McHugh, Jim McFarlane, Kerry Sharp, Cameron Ure, Neil Tocher and James Ferguson. I'd also like to thank Gayle Cunningham and Jo McEwan, for their help with tracking down the right people.

Graham Lironi

Thanks to Susan Christie, Mike Rutterford, Barry Sealey, David Ovens, Gayle Cunningham, Dr Niall MacKenzie, Margaret Coughtrie, Ali Moore and Sara Hunt.

163

Peter Shakeshaft
My contribution to the writing of this book came from my real-time experience as gatekeeper and chief executive of the Archangel syndicate. During that time I made many friends and met many inspiring entrepreneurs. I am grateful to them all for the contribution they made to the success of Archangels and for the provision of many stories . . . only some of which were suitable to be recorded in this book.